PSYCHE AND PERSONALITY

HANI MONTAN

Copyright © 2013 Hani Montan

Author: Hani Montan
Australia, NSW, Panania

Title: Psyche and Personality / Hani Montan

Edition: 1st ed.

Edited by CreateSpace

Printed by CreateSpace
7290 B. Investment Drive
Charleston, SC 29418
USA

ISBN (13): 978 – 1490555225 (paperback & e-book formats)
ISBN (10): 1490555226

Subjects:
Psychology
Personality disorders
Education
Interpersonal relations
Social status

Library of Congress Control Number: 2013912304
CreateSpace Independent Publishing Platform
North Charleston, South Carolina

National Library of Australia (CiP)-Dewey Number: 150

BISAC (category): Nonfiction

Author's earlier books: (available from Amazon.com in paperback and e-book formats)
Thorny Opinion
Dads Gags
Israel vs. America vs. the World
Death by Choice versus Religious Dogma

CONTENTS

INTRODUCTION

Dealing with the subject of psychology is not an easy task, especially because its historical transition from philosophy into science makes it laden with complicated philosophical and scientific terminologies. In this book, I attempt to demystify the subject and thus limit the use of complicated scientific terms and metaphors. However, when the use of a scientific term or metaphor is absolutely necessary, the definition and the context of its use are provided immediately following the relevant paragraph.

Anyone seeking a simplified text on psychology—not one written by a psychologist for other psychologists, which is often the case—should find this book useful. I attempt to help readers to understand the basics of psychology and to develop self-awareness, a tool that can be used as a starting point in the resolution of many common personality disorders. Understanding the basics of consciousness is the first step toward expanding your personal horizons and appreciating the subject and its implications. The book will take you on a journey into psychology, which is probably unlike any you have experienced.

In a world faced with a wide array of issues like unemployment and crime, individuals are constantly searching for someone to blame for disruptions to society. The root of such issues affecting societies around the globe likely lies in the educational and economic systems that fail millions of people on a daily basis. Because the standard school curriculum taught in classrooms across the United States and elsewhere in the Western world is severely lacking in teaching emotional and social intelligences, we are left with a world riddled with widespread bullying, binge drinking, drug use and abuse, violence, delinquency, anxiety, anger, and depression. By ignoring the importance of psychological literacy—and neglecting to provide individuals with the tools needed to develop emotional and social intelligences—society is cultivating a culture devoid of well-adjusted and balanced minds, the impact of which is detrimental for the future.

To combat the problems posed by an absence of emotional and social intelligences among members of society, I attempt to provide readers with an easy-to-understand and enlightening look into the complex field. This book offers an informative yet uncomplicated introduction to the basic components of psychology. Using language a general audience is capable of quickly comprehending, I discuss some of the most common types of personality disorders—such as narcissism, inferiority, and insecurity—and the way the behaviors affect society.

After closely examining the role that human relations, socioeconomics, and education play in the development of these disorders that plague people of various ages, races, and ethnicities, a solution to the problem is to encourage individuals to practice self-awareness. A starting point in the study of psychology is emotional intelligence, the use of self-examination to achieve self-awareness and self-control. Emotional intelligence in turn leads to the development of social intelligence, which is the art of understanding others and how they think. And understanding others is the catalyst for harmonious relationships and better communication between people. Once such intelligences are acquired, individuals become better equipped to respond to a range of situations that occur in everyday life. By making a conscious effort to develop emotional and social intelligences, readers have the opportunity to begin resolving problems caused by personality disorders, to ultimately control impulses, and to cultivate harmonious relationships.

Chapters 1, 2, 3, and 4 provide details of the many components of personality and their impact on social and interpersonal relationships. Chapter 5 deals more specifically with some aspects of psychology and common personality disorders, such as narcissism, insecurity, and inferiority complexes. The remaining chapters deal with other relevant behavioral issues and subjects that have a major impact on human relations.

I hope this book will add to your general knowledge and improve your awareness and understanding of yourself and others. It's a book for reading more than once and one that some readers will use as a reference book.

Editorial overview (October, 2013):

In this manuscript, the author takes on the complex task of presenting the fundamental concepts of psychology in a way that the average reader can understand, benefit from, and apply to daily life. By using simple language, giving detailed explanations of basic terminology, and describing current political and educational situations that could be improved with the application of some of these core concepts, the author has succeeded in his endeavor. As the author had hoped for and anticipated, this work forms a good reference for those who want to dig a little deeper into psychology without becoming overwhelmed by scientific or technical definitions.

ABOUT THE AUTHOR

Hani Montan is an Australian citizen. He is married and has two daughters and one granddaughter.

In 1966 Montan earned a Master of Science degree in civil and industrial engineering.

He has travelled extensively, including studying and working in Iraq, Russia, Algeria, and Australia. To keep abreast of social, managerial, and technical developments, he has studied many subjects, including project management, public relations, environmental protection, social and political science, psychology, human relations, business administration, and philosophy.

Montan worked at Sydney Water as a project engineer and group leader and owned and managed a retail business. It's his engineering instinct, however, that embodies "the power of observation" and gives him the capacity to come to logical conclusions and offer simplified solutions to many problems. Furthermore, the experience he has gained from working with and managing people over many years and his long interest in politics and social studies have given him the motivation to write about many different subjects that might be useful to many readers. His other books (*Thorny Opinion, Dads Gags, Israel vs. America vs. the World*, and *Death by Choice versus Religious Dogma*) are available from Amazon.com and other retailers in both paperback and e-book formats. Other than his humorous book *Dads Gags*, the other books deal with social, political, religious, euthanasia, and other issues, such as climate change and pollution.

In this book, *Psyche and Personality*, he makes a genuine attempt to demystify the subject of psychology to benefit the general reader. Besides studying psychology, his life experience taught him a lot more, which inspired him to write about and simplify such a complex subject. This book deals with the components of personality and personality disorders, such as emotional intelligence, social intelligence, narcissism, insecurity, and inferiority complexes. The book also deals with the deficiency of school education, some aspects of mental health, and other relevant subjects that affect the social environment, such as violence, bullying, drug and alcohol abuse, and family relationships.

Montan grew up in a Christian Orthodox family that had limited devotion to religion. The antireligious tone of his books has its roots in his becoming an atheist at the age of fourteen and his becoming involved in politics at the age of fifteen. A firm believer in a secular system of government, he objects to religious leaders who impose dogmas in their attempt to control the political and social agendas in our civilized society. In secular democracy, religious beliefs should be the privilege of the believer, not an issue in the political domain. Imposing dogmas on others destroys the concept of secular democracy.

He observes that the commercialization of religion has been essential for its growth and survival. And religious leaders have understood for centuries that money is power, and power means control. Control still means everything, mentally, socially, and politically, and contemporary religious leaders now attempt to tangle religion and politics in order to use religion for lobbying purposes. The silent majority understands that allowing the interdependence of religion and politics is a backward step that can lead to religious dominance over a country and the lives of its citizens. The silent majority also understands that backward-looking religious leaders have the desire to take their countries back into the distant past, and some are capable of doing so.

He also observes that believing in myths as absolute facts prevents the mind from analyzing and accepting logic. Religion, therefore, doesn't lend itself to reasoning and open-mindedness. It is in conflict with humankind's enquiring mind, which is constantly searching for answers and will not be satisfied with today's conclusion but strives for a better one tomorrow. Humans are motivated by curiosity to discover and to apply their discoveries to improve their lives and their chances of survival.

His blogs on various subjects can be found at Open Forum website (www.openforum.com.au).

CHAPTER 1

Intelligence - IQ

Definition

Early philosophers preferred to define intelligence as understanding. Mainstream researchers define it as a general mental capability that, among other things, involves the ability to reason, plan, solve problems, think abstractly, comprehend complex ideas, learn quickly, and learn from experience. It is not merely book learning or narrow academic skill or test taking and passing with distinction. Rather, intelligence reflects a broader and deeper capability for comprehending one's surroundings and making sense of things, or figuring out what to do.

There are probably as many definitions of *intelligence* as there are experts who study it. One such definition is that intelligence is the ability to learn about, learn from, understand, and interact with one's environment. This general ability consists of a number of specific abilities that include the following:

- adaptability to a new environment or to changes in the current environment

- capacity for knowledge and the ability to acquire it
- capacity for reason and **abstract thought***
- ability to comprehend relationships between and among ideas
- ability to evaluate and judge
- capacity for original and productive thought

** **Abstract thought** refers to a concept or idea not associated with any specific instance; it can also be thought of as a sketchy summary of the main points of an argument or theory. It's thought that is separated from tangible reality, facts, objects, or specific examples. One who can think abstractly has the ability to represent an object or a scene through description.*

Other definitions of intelligence include the following:

- capacity for learning, reasoning, and understanding and aptitude in grasping truths, relationships, facts, and meanings
- manifestation of a high mental capacity
- the faculty of understanding
- knowledge of an event, circumstance, or received or imparted information
- the gathering or distribution of information

Additional specific abilities might be added to the list, but they would all be abilities allowing a person to learn about, learn from, understand, and interact with the environment. *Environment* in this context doesn't refer to geography or climate. Although it can mean that kind of environment, it has a wider meaning that includes a person's immediate surroundings, including the people around him or her. It can be something as small as a home, the workplace, or a school.

Other definitions of intelligence can be summarized as follows:

- general cognitive problem-solving skills
- a mental ability involved in reasoning, perceiving relationships and analogies, calculating, learning quickly, and so on
- what you do when you don't know what to do
- a hypothetical idea that has been defined as being reflected by certain types of behavior

However, for simplicity, a summary of intelligence could be as follows:

Intelligence is the mental capacity to learn, comprehend, and reason and the ability to deal with various situations. It is also used to describe individuals having great natural ability or talent that is significantly higher than average. So-called intelligent individuals experience mental growth ahead of physical growth and possess the mental process to generate new ideas or concepts or new associations between existing ideas or concepts. Freak individuals with super brains can process complicated tasks at a fast speed.

Some psychologists have divided intelligence into sub-categories. In 2006, in the book *Multiple Intelligences: New Horizons in Theory and Practice* by Howard E. Gardner, a professor in cognition and education at the Harvard Graduate School of Education, Gardner articulates the social, educational, and psychological impacts of his theory of seven multiple intelligences and speculates on how intelligence shows its multifaceted attributes in various forms, such as logical-mathematical, **kinesthetic**, ** musical, interpersonal, intrapersonal, linguistic, spatial, and then he added as newly identified intelligences, naturalistic, and existentialist abilities.

** *Kinesthesis* *is the muscle sense or the sense of movement—the ability to feel movements of the limbs and body. It also implies body language.*

Gardner explores why individuals with strong abilities in certain areas of mathematics, such as algebra or probability theory, do not necessarily possess strengths in other areas of mathematical sciences, such as geometry or topology. He also explores the ways society can take advantage of the theory of multiple intelligences to create a bridge between ethical values and individuals' capacities. Finally he looks at how educators can achieve results by exercising various methods, such as foundational, quantitative, aesthetic, logical, and **existential**, *** to incite the human intellect and enhance the educational impact of the intelligence. He believes that there are many ways that an educator can approach a topic in pursuit of understanding with a methodology that also helps students to think about a problem in a variety of ways, triggering the dynamic process of thought.

*** *Existential methods* are derived from experience or the experience of existence. Such teaching involves experiential content. The word existential relates to the dealing with existence.

Gardner believes efforts need to be made to identify, enhance, and exercise the abilities that help individuals to thrive in the areas that they have been blessed with, irrespective of societal norms. His theory covers various forms of intelligence, such as existential intelligence as a form of computational capacity, and the semantics of each intelligence in relation to intensity, diversity, and locality of these potentials in an individual's characteristics. He provides a simplified and standardized conception of the intelligence development across the life-span of a human being. He examines the topic of memory and its different faculties, such as procedural memory, propositional memory, semantic memory, short- and long-term memories, critical thinking, humanity, and ethics.

Gardner is passionate about striking a balance between ensuring that everyone receives a common education and ensuring that everyone is able to pursue his or her own strengths as far as possible. "To my mind," he states, "a human intellectual competence must entail a set of skills of problem solving—enabling the individual to resolve genuine problems or difficulties that he or she encounters and, when appropriate, to create an effective product—and must also entail the potential for finding or creating problems—and thereby laying the groundwork for the acquisition of new knowledge."

In conclusion, Gardner's book and maybe this humble book are suitable for slow readers who consider the discussed topics to be educational and useful for improving their critical thinking skills. The problem with Gardner's book, however, is that it's very scientific; it's written by a psychologist for psychologists, complete with technical and scientific terminology that makes it difficult for a general reader to follow. His style is understandable, being that Gardner, a professor of cognition and education at Harvard Graduate School of Education, is responsible for producing future teachers and psychologists. On the other hand, the author of this book—being a run-of-the-mill writer who is mainly guided by his basic knowledge of psychology, an eventful life, and extensive experience in dealing with or managing people—has no such responsibility. Howard Gardner's excellent knowledge and writing, however, are a huge inspiration for every writer who is willing to devote time and energy to simplifying the text for the benefit of general readers. Simplicity helps the reader avoid—as much as possible—the need to resort to an encyclopedia or a dictionary.

IQ and Early Learning

Many parents jump to a conclusion about the IQ, or intelligence quotient, of their toddlers by a narrow and subjective observation and without taking into consideration whether the child is an early or late developer. Many children achieve far beyond their capacity by assessments that are based on early subjective observation or even based on a professional test. It is a known fact that developmental delays occur for many reasons, but there are many tools parents can use to encourage their children to grow healthy brains while having fun. From the moment of birth, a baby's brain develops by movement and experience. Taking in the world through the senses, the child develops more brain cells and more connections between the cells. Much research shows that toddlers who are exposed to many different experiences and who are held and carried have larger brains and higher IQs. Research also shows that if toddlers are left to lie down and stay idle with very little movement or human contact, their development is delayed.

To help the child's brain development, it is necessary to provide him or her with good nutrition, especially by breast-feeding, hydration, changing the child's environment, encouraging curiosity, talking and using sign language, creating exposure to music and dance, and so on. Further on, to improve the intellectual performance, the child should have intensive preschool education to ensure his or her orderly development. In kindergarten, the child is exposed to environmental stimulation and receives a start in social intelligence that will help in schooling and life afterward. According to Dr. Craig Ramey of the University of Alabama, the evidence that environmental stimulation could improve IQ and cut the incidence of mental retardation refutes the fashionable view that intelligence is innate, fixed by the genes, and cannot be altered significantly by teaching. There is now substantial evidence that intellectual development can be shaped in a positive sense. Early experience is critical for full development of intellectual capacity. Dr. Ramey and other experts confirm that genes cannot act independently of their environment.

The evidence for the benefits of children's early education is very clear. While such early education may initially appear expensive, in the long run the benefits far outweigh the initial cost, especially when all factors—including juvenile delinquency and mental retardation—are taken into consideration. As the old saying goes, *"If you think education is expensive, you should see the price of ignorance."*

Intelligence Tests

Intelligence is often measured by an IQ test, an aptitude test that assesses an individual's verbal, numerical, reasoning, and learning abilities, as well as planning, problem-solving, and communication skills. The test is only considered useful at an early age of development, before the entrenchment of cultural bias, especially in relation to gender, race, and the social environment. Education assessment, including holistic evidence of performance and achievements, in addition to the test, is considered a more reliable method for measuring intelligence. Intelligence tests do not measure creativity, character, personality, or other important differences among individuals, nor are they intended to.

A number of psychologists have argued that intelligence can be quantified, primarily through testing. In 1905 Alfred Binet and Theodore Simon devised a system for testing intelligence, with scoring based on average mental levels for various age groups. However, the German psychologist L. Wilhelm Stern was the first to coin the term *intelligence quotient*, a figure derived from the ratio of mental age (as determined by the test) to chronological age. Although Stern's method for determining IQ is no longer in common use, the term IQ is still used today to describe the results of several different tests.

IQ is primarily used to measure children's cognitive abilities, such as the ability to learn or understand new situations, to reason through a given problem, and to apply knowledge to their current situations. As a rough guide, psychologists apply the following classifications of IQ:

> **Note:** The following IQ scores are provided by the IQ Test Center. They are the results of a formula based on the number of questions answered correctly on the test. The scores have been further adjusted to account for the differences in capabilities among various age groups. The scores also show the percentage of population in each group:

IQ	Description	Percentage of Population
Over 144	Genius	0.13
133–144	Gifted	2.14
115–129	Above average	13.59
100–114	Higher average	34.14
85–99	Lower average	34.14
70–84	Below average	13.59
55–69	Borderline low	2.14
Below 55	Low	0.13

Lewis Madison Terman, the inventor of the Stanford-Binet IQ test and the initiator of the longitudinal study of children with high IQs, came up with slightly different results and descriptions. His following scores should be noted:

IQ	Description
145 and over	Genius
120 – 144	Exceptional
110 – 119	High average
90 – 109	Average or normal
80 – 89	Dull normal
70 – 79	Borderline deficiency or mild disability
50 – 69	Moderate disability
20 – 49	Severe disability
Below 20	Profound disability

According to the Davidson Institute-Extreme Intellect website, the average IQ is between 85 and 115, which is derived from dividing a person's tested mental age by his or her chronological age and multiplying that number by 100. In Western countries, 25 percent of populations have higher than that, and 25 percent have lower. While there are indicators that a child may be in the high or low range of IQ, an expert like Professor David Palmer (author of *Parents' Guide to IQ Testing and Gifted Education, 2006.*) warns that there are no "sure signs." A designation of "mentally retarded" or "gifted" should be weighed against other factors, such as emotional and social skills, because learning disabilities often exist alongside a high IQ.

Signs that a child's IQ may be lower than average may be walking and talking later than children of the same age. Other signs include poor social skills in play-learn situations with other children or delayed self-care, hygiene, dressing, and feeding skills. As the child grows older, difficulties in learning academic skills and in achieving adequate job skills may also be indicators.

On the other hand, signs that a child's IQ may be higher than normal may be early walking and talking, communication, and social skills. The child may also have a high energy level, show interest in artistic activities, have rapid and complicated language patterns, or show empathy for others and leadership among peers. (Empathy is described further in chapter 2.)

Note: Some children may have both a high IQ and learning difficulties. According to

David Palmer, "children with attention defi-
cit disorder are often in the normal to high
range of IQ. They may be very good at com-
puter games, hear several conversations at
once, and be very active in play but at the
same time seem unfocused, jump from one
activity to another, and score lower than
expected on academic tests."

Today, an average IQ score is considered to be 100, with
deviations based on this figure. While some people are very
smart or very dull, most people cluster around the average.
There are different types of intelligence tests, but they all
measure the same intelligence. Some use words or numbers and require specific cultural knowledge (like vocabulary). Others use shapes or designs and require knowledge
of only simple, universal concepts. Intelligence tests should
not be biased against any race, culture, or gender. The main
criticism of intelligence testing is that it is difficult to ensure
that test items are equally meaningful or difficult for members of different sociocultural groups.

Within the discipline of psychology, various approaches
to human intelligence have been adopted. The **psychometric*** approach is especially familiar to the general public,
as well as being the most researched and by far the most
widely used in practical settings. Individuals differ from
one another in their ability to understand complex ideas,
adapt effectively to the environment, learn from experience, engage in various forms of reasoning, and overcome

obstacles by adopting different thoughts. Although these individual differences can be substantial, intellectual performance can vary on different occasions and should be judged by different criteria. Because of differences in opinion over the definition of intelligence, the concepts of measuring it are varied. Although some clarity has been achieved in its definition, many psychologists and learning theorists have yet to come to a final agreement.

Psychometric: *refers to any branch of psychology concerned with psychological measurements.*

In his book, *IQ and Psychometric Test Workbook: Essential Preparation for Verbal, Numerical and Spatial Aptitude Tests and Personality Tests*, (2011), Philip Carter provides hundreds of practice test questions and answers with explanations. And in his other book, *IQ and Aptitude Tests: Assess Your Verbal, Numerical and Spatial Reasoning Skills*, (2011), he gives four hundred practice questions along with answers, explanations, and a guide to assessing performance.

These books include verbal aptitude tests, numerical aptitude tests, visual aptitude tests, problem-solving tests, personality questionnaires, and advice on adopting the right approach to psychometric testing. Also, the books include tests on word meanings, grammar and comprehension, advanced verbal aptitude, logical analysis, mental arithmetic, numerical sequences, and number problems. The books can help those who are faced with an aptitude or IQ test, as well as anyone who wants to improve his or her verbal and numerical reasoning skills.

In conclusion, psychologist John D. Mayer, in regard to measuring intelligence, said, "I am a great believer that the criterion-report, 'i.e., the ability testing' is the only adequate method to employ. Intelligence is a mental ability and is directly measured only by having people answer questions and evaluating the correctness of those answers."

Heredity and Intelligence

It is generally accepted that intelligence is inherited. While studies show that heredity is an important factor in determining intelligence, it has also been suggested that one's environment (social and natural) is a critical factor in determining the extent of its expression. It is also believed that race and culture play roles in intelligence as well, but so far there is no confirmation that intelligence varies from race to race.

The heredity factor, based on recent studies, revealed that 70 percent of the differences in twins' IQ scores was attributable to inherited traits. Other studies, however, have suggested that only 50 percent of the differences in scores was inherited. Generally, the majority of studies suggest that there is a strong genetic influence on IQ, especially on verbal and relative abilities. Genes determine the quality of intelligence and the ability to integrate and process information. Biologically, it is inherently easier to degrade brain tissue than to create more complex brain tissue. Enhancements in brain structure require long periods of evolutionary selection, in addition to extraneous sources of energy, while brain degradation can happen in a relatively shorter time. There is no evidence to indicate that the environment can increase intelligence to a relatively high level. The level of intelligence determines how well an individual copes with changes in the environment. Environmental factors play a role, and in some instances they are capable of slowing down the mental process more than enhancing it.

The social environment, however, has an influence on the behavioral and developmental aspects of intelligence. Social conditioning, for example, could either suppress hormonal effects or accelerate the natural genetic influence on instinct, desire, urge, and motivation. Knowledge and experience, combined with the genetic makeup of a person, are some of the main components of a personality. (For more on personality, see chapter 3, and for more on knowledge and experience, see chapter 4.)

Besides heredity, emotional learning concerning temperament, gentleness, and empathy versus meanness of spirit and aggression are behavioral elements learned mostly from parents, schools, and the social environment. In many instances, adults tend to treat others the way they were treated by parents and friends in the early stages of their development. Temperament is the typical mood of emotional life. It is generally assumed to be genetically inherited, but it can be conditioned by behavioral methods. (* see **Example** below.)

At birth, the wiring in the brain can result in different temperaments, such as self-consciousness, sensitivity, courage or fearfulness, and shyness or confidence. Each of these scenarios results from how the emotional circuitry affects different people in different ways and to a different degree. The intensity, the speed of triggering, and the duration of the impact are different in different people. The majority of behavior and the pattern associated with all scenarios can be modified by methods of upbringing and through thinking and practicing relative to the social environment. Everyone is a product of nature and nurture. Here it should be emphasized that when thinking is involved, practice is to be taken into consideration. It's extremely difficult to learn to think without practicing.

> *** Example:** We observe diverse reactions of different babies to strangers. The reaction could be either fear followed by panic and screams or a smile and outstretched arms, indicating the desire to be carried or hugged. Another example, in older children, is the shy child who talks much less than a confident child. In each negative scenario, if the child's reactions are not addressed during early childhood, the problem can persist during the teen and adult years. A methodical solution should be found as early as possible to ensure the development of the child's intelligence and emotional intelligence that allows him or her to grow up normally, which, in turn, enables the individual to reach his or her full potential in adulthood. A starting point is for parents to understand and deal with the child's

insecurity and develop methods to make the child feel secure before the problem becomes entrenched in his or her subconscious.

Increasing Intelligence

For the grown-up, there are many ways to increase or amplify intelligence with the help of proven cognitive tools. These include the practice of aiding the memory and using commonsense rules that are intended to increase the probability of solving problems by using creativity techniques and decision-making tools. An increase in one's intelligence level can only result in a better life, health, and standard of living. Many goals can be achieved by the following:

- First is **deep thinking*** to be conscious of what action is needed to reach the objective and to evaluate the consequences of the action to minimize the possibility of a negative outcome.

- Second is determining how to succeed by having an objective, analyzing it, making a decision, and having an alternative method. On observing the outcome of an action, the brain will be capable of using the experience as reference.

- Third, all experiences (good or bad), discoveries, observations, and conclusions reached should be recorded not only for personal benefit but for the benefit of future generations.

- Finally, as stated earlier, to achieve a positive outcome, practice and deep thinking should be taken into consideration. One of the hardest acts is to know how to get rid of the early indoctrination an individual was subjected to. Religious indoctrination, for example, traps people in the box of subjectivity at an early age, which makes it difficult for people to become free thinkers. Setting oneself free from something one didn't choose in the first place requires deep thinking. It is ultimately the individual's knowledge, self-analysis, and critical thinking that can get him or her out of the box and to freedom.

Deep thinking is the thinking beyond what the mind does in its defaults mode. It takes place when the mind is less cluttered with random, meaningless thoughts, worries, and desires, which prevent us from experiencing and exploring the higher levels of consciousness. It is the intellectually disciplined process of actively and skillfully conceptualizing, applying, analyzing, and evaluating information gathered from, or generated by observation, experience, reflection, reasoning, and communication. Deep thinking is how we increase our number of valuable and useful thoughts. Everyone thinks; it is human nature to do so. But deep thinking people attempt to live happily, rationally, without bigotry and prejudice.

It should be pointed out that the links between IQ and emotional intelligence (EI), especially in regard to *motivation*,

** enthusiasm, and dedication play a major role in achievement. They give the emotionally intelligent person the edge in the field of discovery, recognition, acknowledgment, and managing emotions. IQ in this case is a great help in the development of emotional intelligence. Because some people are more capable of developing EI, it is normal for them to have the capacity and suitability for leadership roles, which is a key element of social intelligence. (For more on social intelligence, see chapter 3.)

** *Motivation is the psychological feature that arouses a person to action toward a desired goal. The reason for the action gives purpose and direction to the behavior. According to the Vroom-Yetton contingency model, (1973), "Motivation depends on the size of the reward that is on offer and the likelihood of it being attained."*

The ambitions and productivity of people with a low IQ are limited, especially in the fields of motivation, responsibility, confidence, and emotional and social intelligences. On the other hand, people with a higher IQ and high EI are predictable and socially equipped with a high level of intellectual confidence, commitment, acceptance of responsibility, optimism, and so on. Optimism is the greatest motivator. IQ and EI always work in a complementary way. It's very unusual for a person to have high EI if his or her IQ is very low. The link between EI and IQ can be demonstrated by how a person appeals to emotions to convince someone or uses emotions to function without using logic. Intelligence is about knowing how and why without necessarily knowing what. And it is to know how to motivate each individual differently instead of treating everyone the same way. It's also about understanding and managing the person's own emotions to achieve objectives rather than allowing emotions to control him or her. In regard to the link between IQ and EI, some psychologists tend to devalue the role of women and differentiate between women and men without taking into consideration women's progress, their economic participation, and their current and future social positions. This is when women's progress will lead to a total equality with men after decades of marginalization, oppression, and stereotyping.

Some aspects of human relations, however, relate to the concept of survival of the fittest, such as competition and adversarial interpersonal relationships, which drive humans to have the edge over their fellow humans. In some instances a smarter individual can triumph over the less smart, and in other instances an individual with an average intelligence can be more successful than a genius. This individual, however, likely has a higher level of emotional intelligence, which helps him or her to go through life more easily than the smart one who succeeds at school. It isn't surprising to occasionally come across a genius without personality.

To conclude with the words of Charles Darwin, *"It is not the strongest of the species that survives, nor the most intelligent, but the one most responsive to change."*

CHAPTER 2

Emotional Intelligence

Definition

In his book, *Emotional Intelligence*, (2006), Dr. Daniel Goleman, a Harvard University-trained psychologist and writer for the *New York Times*, wrote; emotional intelligence is measured by the following five main components:

- intrapersonal skills (ability to understand and apply personal emotions)
- interpersonal skills (people skills)
- stress management (ability to handle challenges)
- adaptability (ability to react quickly, appropriately, and efficiently to change)
- general mood (feeling of optimism and happiness)

According to Professor Reuven Bar-On of the University of Texas Medical Branch, the definition of the above components of emotional intelligence is as follows:

- **Intrapersonal skills** consist of emotional self-awareness, assertiveness, self-regard, independence, and self-actualization. These skills provide one with the ability to respect and accept himself or herself and relate to a person's ability to feel fulfilled and satisfied with himself or herself regardless of perceived strengths and weaknesses.

- **Interpersonal skills** consist of empathy, connection with others, and social responsibility. These skills give a person the ability to establish and maintain mutually satisfying relationships that are characterized by intimacy and by giving and receiving affection. They allow one to establish and maintain positive and satisfying relationships with others.

- **Stress management** consists of stress tolerance and impulse control.

- **Adaptability consists** of problem solving, reality testing, and flexibility.

- **General mood** consists of happiness and optimism.

In 1990 psychologists Peter Salovey and John D. Mayer were the leading researchers on emotional intelligence. They published the influential article "Emotional Intelligence" in the journal *Imagination, Cognition, and Personality*. They defined emotional intelligence as "the subset of social intelligence that involves the ability to monitor one's own and others' feelings and emotions, to discriminate among them, and to use this information to guide one's thinking and actions." Salovey and Mayer proposed a model that identified four different factors of emotional intelligence: the perception of emotions, the ability to reason using emotions, the ability to understand emotions, and the ability to manage emotions. A brief explanation of each follows.

Perceiving emotions: The first step in understanding emotions is to accurately perceive them. In many cases, this might involve understanding nonverbal signals such as body language and facial expressions.

Reasoning with emotions: The next step involves using emotions to promote thinking and cognitive activity. Emotions help prioritize what we pay attention to and react to; we respond emotionally to things that garner our attention.

Understanding emotions: The emotions that we perceive can carry a wide variety of meanings. If someone is expressing angry emotions, the observer must interpret the cause of the anger and what it might mean. For example, if your boss is acting angry, it might mean that he is dissatisfied with your work. Or it could be that he got a speeding ticket on his way to work that morning or that he's been fighting with his wife.

Managing emotions: The ability to manage emotions effectively is a key part of emotional intelligence. Regulating emotions, responding appropriately, and responding to the emotions of others are all important aspects of emotional management.

In short and for simplicity, however, it could be said that emotional intelligence is the art of self-examination to achieve *self-awareness** and self-control. Understanding oneself leads to understanding others and, ultimately, social intelligence. Understanding others and how they think is the catalyst for harmonious relationships and better communication between people. In this context, it may be necessary to have a basic understanding of psychology and the most common personality disorders. (For more on personality disorders, see chapter 5.) This, in turn, can help individuals to use their own mental power to overcome minor psychological problems as part of the process of developing emotional intelligence and, as a result, achieve resistance against manipulation and the herd mentality. The acquired knowledge could then be applied to the detection of negative influences aimed at individuals and groups, which constitute the major forces causing conflict in human relations worldwide. Above all, emotional intelligence entails intellectual honesty, especially by acknowledging when one is wrong or lucky.

** **Self-awareness** is one of the difficult aspects of personal achievement, as it entails digging into the subconscious, discovering learned complexes, and bringing them into the conscious mind to enable them to be resolved. It leads to self-control, impulse control, positive thinking, and optimism. According to psychologists, a person who is self-aware is aware of his or her mood and any thoughts about that mood. Self-awareness also equips the person with awareness of others (a key element of social intelligence) and helps him or her become less susceptible to manipulation. It leads to better communication, especially when it develops to a stage in which the person learns what the other person thinks, known as the stage of the widened personal horizon. Self-awareness is a fundamental element of emotional intelligence and mood control. It is finding balance in one's feelings and avoiding pathological extremes. It is the key to controlling worries, mood swings, anxiety disorders, phobias, obsessions, compulsions, panic attacks, and so on. It eliminates the need for therapy, except for chronic symptoms and major depression.*

Behavioral self-assessment depends on a person's own psychological energy, knowledge, and experience. These factors enable him or her to discover personality disorders and complexes he or she developed since birth. With additional studies and experience, self-assessment could also become the key to the ability of observing and assessing others. A disciplined personal response to a range of situations and experiences—the control of one's impulses—is an essential element of successful interpersonal relationships. The forming of impulses and personality, except for the hereditary elements, normally starts from the day of birth, when the first contact is made with the external world. Behavioral conditioning to control the impulses also commences immediately after birth. Parents, nurses, friends, relatives, and caregivers strive to ensure the child's adaptation to the external environment and the conditioning toward social conformity.

This is also the time when conflict between genetics and conditioning begins, and the conscious, the subconscious, the ego, and the superego begin to form. When one has grown up, the ego could be manifested in the person's projected image and a feeling of insecurity, while the superego is usually manifested in the person's level of selfishness and a feeling of inferiority. (For more on narcissism and other personality disorders, see chapter 5.) People with lesser emotional intelligence are generally the main target for manipulation and indoctrination, especially by some sinister politicians and religious leaders. Self-awareness and the awareness of others could be the key to resisting the herd mentality, mass psychology, and mind control.

Teaching self-awareness means making people understand that their thoughts relate to their state of mind and that positive thinking can overcome many negative emotions. This includes the following:

- First, one way to deal with depression and sadness is by socializing.

- Second, isolation, passive immersion in sadness, and constant worry about depression make the situation worse.

- Third, distracting oneself from the cause of the blues lessens their impact.

- Fourth, in any relationship there are advantages and disadvantages or negatives and positives. When the focus is on the negatives and the disadvantages, the relationship is doomed. On the other hand, the relationship can survive and prosper when the focus is on the positives and the advantages.

- Ultimately, the solution for many of our ills is optimism, self-confidence, and self-awareness. And in each of the above scenarios, emotional intelligence plays the starring role. The logical anchor of human relations should be **empathy**** that is founded on give-and-take, "caring and sharing," and win-win bases rather than on a winner-takes-all philosophy.

** **Empathy** *is the projection of one's emotion or consciousness into another being. It leads to caring, compassion, and healthy altruism. The more empathic a person is, the more he or she believes in moral principles, justice, and equality.*

Some psychologists metaphorically describe empathy as a function of the heart, when it is actually a function of the mind. Empathy as defined above is the projection of one's emotions or consciousness onto another person and the feeling of compassion and understanding. It's possible that the use of metaphors is intended to help the average reader comprehend the meaning of the concept. It should be made clear, however, that terms such as "the feeling of the heart," "guts feeling," are used figuratively, not literally. It's understandable that it's sometimes difficult to separate psychology from philosophy, but in failing to do so, we overlook the fact that the heart and the guts are mechanical organs—the heart is for pumping blood, and the guts are organs for processing food. The heart and the guts don't think; thinking and consciousness occur in the brain, which controls all bodily functions by signals traveling in both directions between the organs and the brain.

> **Note:** As a diversion from the above, it was discovered that there is actually a physical link between the immune system and the central nervous system. This contact allows the nerve cells to release neurotransmitters to regulate the immune cells. The signals travel in both directions between the cells, rather than through the brain. It was also discovered that emotions play a major role in the functions of the autonomic nervous system, and this, in turn, affects the immune system. The nervous system regulates everything, such as the secretion of hormones and insulin and the levels of blood pressure.

In addition to the above definitions of emotional intelligence, there are many others that are stated by different researchers:

- David Caruso: "It is very important to understand that emotional intelligence is not the opposite of intelligence; it is not the triumph of heart over head—it is the unique intersection of both."

- Peter Salovey and John Mayer: "We define emotional intelligence as the subset of social intelligence that involves the ability to monitor one's own and others' feelings and emotions, to discriminate among them, and to use this information to guide one's thinking and actions."

- John Mayer: "Emotional intelligence is the ability to process emotional information, particularly as it involves the perception, assimilation, understanding, and management of emotion."

On other aspects of emotional intelligence and its importance, psychologists have proposed the potential benefits and offered critical analysis of differing theoretical models. The following quotes are just a sampling of what has been written on the topic of emotional intelligence:

- John Gottman: "In the last decade or so, science has discovered a tremendous amount about the role emotions play in our lives. Researchers have found that even more than IQ, your emotional awareness and abilities to handle feelings will determine your success and happiness in all walks of life, including family relationships."

- Reuven Bar-On: "Emotional intelligence is an array of non-cognitive capabilities, competencies, and skills that influence one's ability to succeed in coping with environmental demands and pressures."

- Peter Salovey and John Mayer: "People in good moods are better at inductive reasoning and creative problem solving."

- John Mayer: "An emotion occurs when there are certain biological, certain experiential, and certain cognitive states that all occur simultaneously."

In regard to his own experience of mental distress and emotional clarity during a college calculus exam, on the subjects of "impulse control, positive thinking, and optimism," Daniel Goleman, in his book, *Emotional Intelligence*, (2006), wrote,

When emotions overwhelm concentration, what is being swamped is the mental capacity cognitive scientists call "working memory," the ability to hold in mind all information relevant to the task at hand. What occupies working memory can be as mundane as the digits that compose a telephone number or as complicated as the intricate plot lines a novelist is trying to weave together. Working memory is an executive function par excellence in mental life, making possible all other intellectual efforts, from speaking a sentence to tackling a knotty logical proposition. The prefrontal cortex executes working memory—and, remember, the prefrontal cortex is where feelings and emotions meet. When the limbic circuitry that converges on the prefrontal cortex is in the thrall of emotional distress, one cost is in the effectiveness of working memory: we can't think straight, as I discovered during that calculus exam.

On the subject of hope and determination, he wrote the following:

> Hope made all the difference. The response by students with high levels of **hope***** was to work harder and think of a range of things they might try that could bolster their final grade. Students with moderate levels of hope thought of several ways they might up their grade but had far less determination to pursue them. And, understandably, students with low levels of hope gave up on both counts, demoralized.

*** **Hope** here relates to optimism rather than unfounded dogmatic beliefs. In religious terms, based on **metaphysics, ****** hope relates to the promise of the afterlife and the eternity, or the belief that the next life will be better. It is a pie in the sky that the hope of a cancer-stricken religious person who is expecting that God will intervene, or that praying to a certain saint will get him or her cured. But if somehow recovery or remission does take place, the individual will broadcast it as divine intervention. The miracle will be claimed even if the original diagnosis was made by human error, and the person will ignore the role that positive thinking or other treatment methods may have played.

**** **Metaphysics** is a type of philosophy that attempts to use a broad concept to define reality and our understanding of it. Generally, it seeks to explain elements and features of reality that are not easily discovered or experienced in our daily life and are beyond the physical world and our immediate senses. It uses arguments based on human terms rather than logic that is tied to human sensory perception of the objective world. It contradicts the laws of physics, which are proven and understood.

When hope is based on optimism, success is predictable rather than fictitious. Optimistic people don't believe in getting help through prayer; they find it in themselves with inner conviction and strength to overcome problems to succeed. For enlightened and scientifically oriented people, miracles are in the realm of fantasy, and optimism relates to self-confidence and the use of common sense, which trump any belief in supernatural fairy tales that deal with speculations and mysteries. (For more on miracles and mysteries, see chapter 2 of my book *Death by Choice versus Religious Dogma*.)

The opposite of optimism is pessimism, including feelings of apathy and defeatism. These are driven by a negative outlook of hopelessness and despair caused mainly by the feeling of incompetency. When a person believes in his or her inadequacy and inability to carry out a task, he or she becomes the victim of his or her own beliefs.

Development of optimism and confidence should start from childhood. Early mentoring by parents and quality teachers is essential in overcoming pessimism and despair, which are common problems that have negative impact on a person's productivity and, in turn, the productivity of the whole country. Parents' role in developing successful children requires two major efforts. First is building children's self-confidence. Second is helping children avoid the wrong friends. (For more on self-confidence and the wrong friends, see below.)

Self-Confidence

Self-confidence has two components: efficiency and self-esteem. Efficiency is mastering skills and reaching goals that are relevant to those skills. It leads a person to accept difficult challenges and remain strong in the face of adversity. Efficiency complements self-esteem, which is, in part, the quality of dealing and coping with life, work, and other people that makes a person happy and more charismatic. Self-esteem is about how much the individual values himself or herself and how much he or she feels other people value him or her. Self-esteem is important because accepting oneself as he or she really is can affect his or her mental stability and behavior. Feeling good about oneself and in control of his or her life makes friends feel good about him or her. In general, happiness comes from a person's perception that he or she is approved of and accepted by others. It also comes from positive thinking and one's sense that he or she possesses the ability to succeed. Without positive thinking and the perceived ability to achieve, one cannot build self-confidence, and a lack of self-confidence causes anxiety and feelings of failure.

Self-confidence can be built through effort and determination to succeed. One should always remember that low self-confidence and negativity are destructive. It is necessary to do what one believes is right and not to do things to appease or please others. One must also have the ability to admit mistakes and learn from them, rather than attempting to cover them up. And one should remember that one has true self-confidence when he or she believes he or she is able to succeed and is committed to success, even if he or she may occasionally fail or not get rewarded. Self-esteem, on the other hand, depends on the person's social network and all the activities he or she participates in. It also relates to other factors, such as one's psychological and physical health. Positive psychological health often overcomes physical health problems, whereas negative body image, depression, and low self-esteem produce the opposite outcome.

When mentors, parents, and teachers address teenagers directly, they should make them conscious of the fact that while they are growing up, their self-esteem can be affected by the discovery of their sexuality, puberty, body transformation, gender, and so on. Their self-awareness of this passing phase can help them focus on their physical activities and their social and academic achievements, which are essential elements for building self-esteem. Ideally, these factors will be complemented by the right environment, both at home and in school. Part of the environment is the friends they choose, and parents may be the best people to help them choose good friends that will support and enhance their academic and social life. Keeping the right company at this age when they are highly impressionable can affect the rest of their lives. To enhance their academic and social lives, they should be encouraged not to hang around with the wrong friends. Bad friends can be destructive to their future and their potential.

The Wrong Friends

In addressing the teenager directly, a teacher or a mentor can emphasize the following: Although your parents are your best friends, being with them day in, day out can get boring. Everybody needs a friend or friends to socialize, have fun, or play sports with. But it's important to know that after a while, subconsciously you will embrace your friends' thinking and mimic their behavior. Which would you choose—friends that will make you a better person or friends that will make you a worse person? There are friends who will change you into a peaceful and successful person, and there are friends who will change you into a drug taker, a binge drinker, and an antisocial person. You have contrasting choices; one will lead you into success, and the other could make you a failure.

Being human, you absorb information from the world around you, and you adapt to this world. Your friends are part of the world that you're choosing. They play a major role in how you interact with the world. Your future is in part shaped by their influence. Now stop and think: Are the friends you're hanging around with going to enhance your future or hinder it?

There are signs you can look for to decide whether certain individuals are the friends you want around for many years or maybe forever. The first thing to look for when choosing friends is their compatibility with your upbringing. At first glance, you can tell which individuals you want to be associated with. This will be apparent in the way they dress, the way they talk, and the way they behave. Do they gossip, bully others, or skip school? Are their remarks racist, rude, or hurtful? You want to enhance and further advance your positive qualities instead of destroying them. A motivated person who has ambitions and goals must know that bad friends will prevent him or her from achieving those ambitions. Hanging around with good friends, on the other hand, can put you on the right track. At the very least, these friends are not going to distract you or destroy your life. But hanging around with the wrong friends can cause you to lose track and lose your way. You must therefore choose what is best for you—friends can bring out the best in you.

Bad friends present themselves as kind and caring people when at the same time they won't hesitate to stab you in the back. These so-called friends are masters in the art of deception. Bad friends or even relatives are the ones who try to promote themselves at your expense, because they're afflicted with insecurity or even an inferiority complex. A bad friend is the one who is excessively jealous, envious, and often dishonest. A bad friend is the one who doesn't believe in give-and-take or mutual benefit.

Instead of trying to correct bad friends, you have to learn when and how to end a bad friendship. Leaving bad friends and finding better ones is not easy because it's natural to want to keep your old friends, but your deep thinking and gradual maturity will tell you when it's time. Only your mind can tell you what the best solution is. In many instances, the solution can be simple, especially when it is obvious that your current friends are bringing you down, and you're getting no benefit from the relationship. Only you can decide, and if you're lucky enough to have good parents, they are the best assets to guide you through.

Parents on the other hand, can help protect their children from bad friendships when they observe the first negative change in their children or behavior that is in conflict with their upbringing. The first thing the parents should do is closely examine the friends who are having a negative effect on the children's personality. Initially when parents criticize their children's friends, the children react strongly; this is a sign that the children are totally devoted and have surrendered to their friends. It's a natural reaction; a person will always defend his or her choice. Parents in this situation should refrain from criticizing their children's friends. Criticism will not be effective and may even drive the children into stronger friendship with the same friends. It's a natural thing for parents to want to protect their children and for children to defend the friends who accept and embrace them.

In this situation, to avoid alienating the children, parents should refrain from constant nagging. Instead, occasionally parents can explain to their children that friends who are often in trouble can get them in trouble as well. Also parents can state directly that they don't want them hanging around with this type of friend. When children show signs of responding positively or actually changing, parents should follow up with rewards for reinforcement. Parents should understand that children go through stages, and one of these stages is rebelliousness. How easily parents forget their own childhood and adolescence! Most likely the mistakes the children are making are the same mistakes the parents made.

The Education System

According to UNICEF, the mission of The Convention on the Rights of the Child is to advocate for the protection of children's rights, help meet children's basic needs, and expand children's opportunities to reach their full potential. The Convention on the Rights of the Child is a universally agreed-upon set of nonnegotiable standards and obligations that can also be called human and civil rights. These rights are founded on respect for the dignity and worth of each individual, regardless of race, color, gender, language, religion, opinions, origins, wealth, birth status, or ability and therefore apply to every human being everywhere.

In many civilized countries, education starts at the pre-school level, where it is becoming routine to make children have a strong sense of identity, be connected and contribute to learning and their world, have a strong sense of well-being, and be confident individuals and effective communicators. Teaching social and emotional skills should continue through to year twelve. The curriculum should coincide with the age and the grade of students.

The learning process is ideal if it uses brainstorming sessions, discussion, and classroom participation to find solutions to problems. Lecturing about values is not enough; teachers must demonstrate how to practice them. Teaching the practice of values leads to development of character.

For a secure and prosperous future, countries should be able to develop children's creativity, emotional intelligence, and social intelligence through the following methods:

- making them feel safe and supported
- making them autonomous and independent
- giving them knowledge
- teaching them interaction with others and developing team spirit and fairness

Furthermore, lessons about well-being (healthy living) and respect for the environment must be assigned a high priority. A country's progress and prosperity cannot be achieved without serious investment in child care, even if the country is in a recession or a financial crisis. And child care cannot be achieved without caregivers who are well qualified for the job. Unfortunately, in many countries the qualifications of caregivers are well below what is required. Their pay, too, is low, and this limits the schools' ability to attract people that are suitable for the task.

In a complex society, children's psychological development is an essential element for societal harmony. For example, teaching children at an early age the concepts of give-and-take, mutual benefit, live and let live, and win-win rather than winner takes all can help their training in conflict resolution, which eventually leads to social stability. Additionally, teaching children at an early age boosts their prospects for life, especially in the development of their vocabulary. Children growing up with educated parents acquire good knowledge of language and a rich vocabulary for conversation. Disadvantaged children, especially those from low-income families, miss out if they are not given the opportunity to learn such at school, which causes half of the country's children to be left behind.

Without the government's early intervention and investment, the vocabulary gap leads to a school achievement gap. That, in turn, can mean that while some go on to college, others drop out without even learning how to read. For the country, the cost of school failure is huge, as it leads to unemployment, crime, and community disruption.

Psychologists generally agree that the most important time for intervention is in the first five years of life, when the brain is developing quickly and interactions with adults matter so much to children's developing sense of who they are and their language development. Unfortunately, the consequences of lack of funding for education are not immediately detectable—and because of this lack of vision, politicians are not interested in giving education the priority it deserves.

Emotional learning starts in early life and continues throughout childhood, when good habits are developed and reinforced by repetition of messages from parents and teachers.

In his book, *Emotional Intelligence*, Daniel Goleman, (2006), writes,

> The first three or four years of life are a period when the toddler's brain grows to about two thirds its full size and evolves in complexity at a greater rate than it ever will again. During this period key kinds of learning take place more readily than later in life—emotional learning foremost among them. During this time severe stress can impair the brain's learning centers (and so be damaging to the intellect).

Children have the capacity to learn, be creative, and use their imaginations; they have commitment and enthusiasm and are endowed with the power of curiosity. When embraced by schools and society, all these characteristics can be directed toward further learning about interacting with others and contributing to modern and future technologies. Development of modern technologies largely depends on many experts applying their multiple skills, working together as a team to produce extraordinary software, a gadget, space technology, or a robot for manufacturing and universal use. This is when corroboration and interpersonal relations come to the fore to design and produce an item for the service of humanity.

At the time of starting school, the child's capacities and his or her emotional intelligence should be enhanced by quality teaching methods. Setting suitable professional standards for teachers is one of the biggest problems facing civilized societies, because a minimum standard is not good enough for an optimum result. Striving for higher standards, together with appropriate remuneration (to attract better-quality professionals) and higher entry marks to universities, is extremely important. Good teachers, as social engineers, are so important to the country's future; their marks for entry into a university shouldn't be lower than the entry marks for engineers. A good education system largely depends on a believing and committed government that allocates high priority to the country's education system. The government must understand that low-quality education is detrimental to the nation's future and that high-quality teaching cannot be achieved without good-quality teachers.

Teaching generally should be treated as one of the country's most important professions, and teachers' qualifications and salaries should be made one of the government's highest priorities. Teachers play a major role in children's developmental psychology, especially in reinforcing positive behavioral trends and detecting and dealing with negative trends before they become entrenched in the subconscious. In both instances, the social and economic benefits to the nation could be immeasurable if only governments would allocate proper resources. Early intervention could be the best way to overcome the costly mental illnesses, antisocial behaviors, and crimes in the country.

Teachers' and parents' knowledge is the key to making future leaders who are equipped with mental, physical, and psychological energies. This could be achieved by focusing on developing children's drive, impulse control, empathy, **anger management**, * commitment, and passion for achievement. Investing in teaching and children's developmental psychology throughout their schooling can benefit the country. Positive outcomes will come from social maturity, social stability, and the mental energy of an army of high-spirited, inspired, and highly productive generations.

* **Anger management:** *Some anger is a necessary part of our survival; however, when it becomes destructive, it can lead to major problems at work and in personal relationships. If anger is a negative emotion, it can make life miserable. The instinctive and natural way to express anger is to respond aggressively. Anger is a natural, adaptive response to threats;*

it often becomes aggressive. This is when it must be understood and managed.

A variety of conscious and unconscious processes exists for dealing with angry impulses, such as expressing assertively, suppressing feelings, and calming. Being assertive—not aggressive—is a healthier way to express anger. Assertiveness doesn't mean being pushy or demanding; it means being respectful of oneself and others.

Pathological expressions of anger—such as getting back at people directly or indirectly, constantly putting others down, criticizing every-thing, and making cynical comments about others—don't leave a person with many friends. The purpose of anger management is to reduce emo-tional feelings and the physical reactions. It should be easy to remember that anger doesn't solve problems and ultimately doesn't result in feeling better; it results in feeling worse.

Understanding common human behavior and aspirations could lead to better interpersonal relations. Interpersonal relations that are based on religious slogans of "an eye for an eye" or "turn the other cheek" are no longer appli-cable in the twenty-first century simply because the "eye for an eye" concept promotes the feeling of aggression and revenge, while "turn the other cheek" promotes the pathetic act of surrender. Today, far removed from reli-gious hocus-pocus, civilized countries deal with human relations on the basis of "one's freedom ends where oth-ers' freedom begins." The laws coincide and are based on the prevailing social tolerance and rehabilitation.

Interpersonal relations also entail teaching children to judge others not by their failures, but by their successes, because failure is an essential element of learning. Thus children feel comfortable learning by experience and refrain from being judgmental, knowing they could be in a similar predicament one day.

Emotional development starts in early childhood. Emotionally intelligent parents and quality teachers are capable of producing well-balanced children who have the potential to improve—not only the society but the quality of the education and the political systems of the country. Emotional intelligence leads to emotional stability, a most important quality that results in using common sense and self-discipline more than using brainpower.

Allowing children to surrender to feelings of helplessness and depression or to adopt a pessimistic outlook instead of being highly motivated and confident with an optimistic outlook can have devastating consequences. Children must be equipped with the ability to change things around when they face adversity.

Here it is worth mentioning the Seattle experiment called Roots of Empathy (first launched in 1996–1997, in Ontario, Canada), an exercise that involves bringing a seven-month-old baby to a kindergarten classroom for the purpose of building more peaceful and caring societies by increasing the level of empathy in children. The program was also adopted in California, New York, and parts of Washington. The idea behind it is that encounters with a baby help kids observe the baby's development and learn to label his or her feelings. The students then reflect on why the baby is either happy or sad and discuss their own similar feelings. At the heart of the program is a mission to decrease aggressive behavior patterns at an early age and therefore curb bullying. (For more on bullying, see chapter 6.)

According to Kim Schonert-Reichl, (1999), a professor at the University of British Columbia who has studied the effects of Roots of Empathy, the program offers teachers a springboard to talk about emotions and helps children learn to identify emotions, become self-aware, and develop relationship skills. A 2011 study in the journal *Child Development* looked at research involving 270,000 students, comparing those who'd participated in social and emotional learning programs like Roots of Empathy with those who had not. The findings showed that students who received the training not only increased their social and emotional skills but also increased their scores on standardized achievement tests by eleven percentage points.

In their book *The Handbook of Emotional Intelligence: Theory, Development, Assessment, and Application at Home, School and in the Workplace*, (2000), Reuven Bar-On and James D. A. Parker evaluate reliable methods for assessing emotional intelligence and provide guidelines for applying the principles of EI in a variety of settings. The book is suitable for businesses, psychologists, teachers, and students alike. It deals with personal intelligence, practical intelligence, and other related subjects and explains developmental methods and behavioral observations in a practical way that suits the educational programs in emotional intelligence and social intelligence.

Another book worth mentioning is *Raising Emotionally Intelligent Teenagers: Guiding the Way for Compassionate, Committed, Courageous Adults*, (2000), by Maurice J. Elias, Steven E. Tobias, and Brian S. Friedlander. This book helps parents, schools, and workplaces to have emotionally intelligent youths who are not only knowledgeable, responsible, and nonviolent, but also compassionate, committed, and productive. The expertise of the authors in developmental psychology and behavioral knowledge shines through. The authors show parents practical ways to use and balance their love and discipline as well as ways to build their children's confidence and make them feel that they belong to school and family. Guiding youths to be useful to themselves and society is a serious challenge, but the outcome is rewarding. Above all, the book teaches both parents and their children the principles of give-and-take and "sharing is caring."

Social and emotional education will ultimately produce better leaders and politicians than those the world currently must live with. In the current political environment, many leaders and politicians around the world are chosen based on lies, deception, and manipulation. Some are outright dishonest, self-serving, and corrupt. If these leaders and politicians were well schooled and had developed properly and adequately, especially in the areas of conflict resolution and the give-and-take principle, the world would be a better place instead of a place in conflict, driven by superegos, dogmas, domination, and excessive greed.

The curriculum, too, must be addressed to ensure that literacy, mathematics, science, and emotional development are given the highest priority. Focus should be placed on ensuring children's psychological development, implementing highly effective practices including experimentation, and making sure teachers themselves are experts in the subjects they teach. As it stands, many teachers have little confidence or preparation for teaching to a standard that meets the needs of the present and the future.

Many teachers and parents are not well equipped to deal with children's lack of confidence during adversity and their inability to turn things around rather than surrendering to despair and helplessness. This is when teachers' qualifications for acting as mentors in psychology and emotional literacy become critical. Additionally, mentoring and consulting parents is also necessary, as parents' emotions have great impact on their children's development. Parents' impulse control and patience, for example, are essential elements in a child's evolution.

In addition to improving teachers' qualifications, the government should provide free education to all citizens. Free education is a human rights issue, and it's the pathway for everybody to reach his or her potential and ultimately for the country to achieve higher productivity. Taxpayers' money should never be diverted to private and religious schools if that means depriving public and disadvantaged schools of proper funding. (For more on private and religious schools, see below under "School Dropouts" and "Religion's Impact on Psychology.")

Children's curiosity and eagerness to learn should be encouraged at every opportunity. Children observe and interact with their environment. They perceive things as presented to them. They develop emotional habits, learn to recognize and manage feelings, and learn empathy or antipathy directly from their home environment and schools, mainly through interaction with their parents, siblings, and other students. Children who are happy and well cared for are likely to be successful in developing confidence, self-control, and effective social skills. Miserable and neglected children, on the other hand, are likely to fail and have lower social skills. Methods of bringing up children have a major impact on the formation of personality, emotional intelligence, and social intelligence.

Unfortunately, today, the diminishment of family life and the family structure as a result of domestic violence, separation and divorce, or financial necessity is exposing children to negative temptation, maladjustment, and delinquency. The vulnerability of children is becoming a major social problem. Many children are growing up without family bonds and without supervision. Neglect is causing them to go astray and become a burden on society and the country's economy. Therefore, schools and teachers are needed to fill the gap and address the psychological development of children. If a school is unable to fill the gap, an unpleasant outcome should be expected. For social stability, the government's focus and funding should take into consideration this reality.

Many Western countries are still living in the past, when the family was a solid unit, children were well disciplined, and religions were strong enough to enforce morality, obedience, conformity, and values. Since the desire for individuality and independence began to influence the social structure, the family unit has begun to disintegrate. This process has been aggravated by the younger generation's abandonment of religion due to its irrelevant dogmatic idealism, its hypocrisy, and its conflict with science. These facts dictate that the school must now serve as social armor, especially for neglected kids and kids from low-income backgrounds. Unfortunately, governments, instead of increasing funding for disadvantaged and other public schools, are reducing funding or diverting money to religious and private schools, where it's not needed. In many instances this produces further negative outcomes due to indoctrination and subjectivity. More funds instead are also going to groups with less need and that are less critical to the country's economic survival and prosperity.

Worse yet, a huge amount of money is wasted on military establishments for interventions around the world. The money is used for fighting expensive and unnecessary wars in other countries, where many innocent people are killed—some as a result of religious wars or wars to fight enemies created by the US empire with its expansionist policy. The key to any country's progress and prosperity depends largely on the strength of its education system and its infrastructure. A good education system cannot be achieved without high-quality teachers and more emphasis on developmental psychology. To attract better-quality students to the teaching profession, it is necessary for universities to require higher entry marks and for employers to offer graduates a rate of pay that is appropriate to their task.

In the United States, for example, a study in July 2011, on teachers' training was conducted by the National Council on Teacher Quality, an independent research and advocacy group. The report looked at teaching programs in more than six hundred institutions and found what it called "an industry of mediocrity."

Among the conclusions were the following: Just one of every four programs restricts admissions for teaching candidates to the top half of college students. And about 70 percent of all programs are not providing elementary teacher candidates with sufficient and current reading training. The report is about 200,000 teachers who come out of teacher training every year and teach 1.5 million kids during that first year. It argues that most teacher-training institutions don't take training seriously, as if it's not really their mission to train teachers. Therefore, when teachers go into their first year of teaching, they're inadequately pre-pared. The problem stems from the fact that it's very easy to become a teacher. To emphasize the point, only a quar-ter of teacher-training institutions restrict the admission to the top half of the class, and the rest will accept anybody from the bottom half of the class.

This problem is common in many countries that don't take education seriously enough to bring it into the twenty-first century. The national curriculum in most countries consists of a list of subjects prescribed for each grade of education, each with an allotted number of hours per week or year. The overall aims for each level are suggested, together with the objectives and content for each subject.

The 1990 curriculum in France aims for better objectives but still doesn't meet the requirement, especially because it has no specific program or number of hours devoted to teaching emotional and social intelligences. It suggests the following general aim: "Elementary school education is to ensure the acquisition of the basic elements and tools of knowledge: oral and written expression, reading, and arithmetic. It stimulates the development and improvement of a child's intelligence, emotional development, artistic sensibility, and manual and physical skills." In this curriculum, French language and social studies were allotted between ten and thirteen hours weekly; mathematics, science, and technology were allotted six to ten hours; and physical and artistic education were allotted six to eight hours. The flexibility of hours allowed the introduction of foreign language instruction in many schools.

The standardized and subject-based curriculum in France is reinforced by assessment that determines whether students will be promoted to the next grade. This assessment places greatest emphasis on language and mathematics. About 10 percent of all students repeat the first grade of primary school. Assessment methods tend to be of the teacher-centered, whole-class type. The standard in France is that all children should acquire knowledge of grammatical structures as well as precision in written and oral expression. Teachers support these values and often resist central advice to focus on the individual student. In contrast to practices in Germany and the United States, textbooks are not prescribed by the state. Assessment is mainly controlled by individual teachers, though decisions must be justified to a council of teachers in the school. National testing, introduced in 1989, aims to provide more information for teachers and parents rather than to construct public league tables (public reporting of test results) of school performance. (For more on quality teachers, see below.)

Generally in Western countries, there is only a token mention or little emphasis on children's development of emotional and social intelligences. This is when the education system must address—and attempt to counter—children's feelings of pessimism, helplessness, and depression. Most of these feelings are generated in the family environment, leaving the schools to fill the gap. Children are affected by divorce and disharmony. With at least 50 percent of couples either divorced or living in conflict, it is easy to see the negative social impact. And it doesn't end there: emotional scars left unaddressed have a negative effect on the country's productivity and health care costs.

Emotional scars could be caused by parental neglect, rejection, divorce or separation, bullying at school, unsuitable foster care, and so on. When the domestic environment is not conducive to a resolution and there is no prospect of getting professional help, the school, counselors, and teachers who are equipped with knowledge of developmental psychology become the last and maybe only resort for helping children and teenagers overcome these traumas. Children with emotional scars usually display a fear of failure and fear of rejection. They are typically unable to relate to others and often exhibit negative emotional reactions and outbursts. In some instances, traumatized children and teenagers need professional help. Unfortunately, governments fail to allocate appropriate resources by misdirecting funds to much lower priorities. Neglecting mental health could save money in the short term, but in the long run, the cost to the community is huge.

It should be remembered that when a social or psychological trend sets in and the country doesn't respond with urgency, it could take a long time—possibly generations—to correct it. Something else to remember is that a maladjusted generation may in turn produce an equally bad or worse generation, which is to the detriment of the country.

At school, teaching emotional skills and the basics of psychology is necessary. Subjects taught can include self-awareness, conflict resolution, motivation, positive thinking, communication, decision making, critical thinking, optimism versus pessimism, overcoming adversity, and so on. It should be emphasized that success cannot be achieved without optimism. Failing to develop children's social skills is a pathway to an increased number of school dropouts, which is a pathway to the country's decline.

Through a problem-solving approach and instruction in emotional and social intelligences that is designed to nurture rather than instruct, children are enabled to develop self-awareness and social skills. Teaching at schools should aim at instilling in children self-confidence, self-understanding, and understanding of others, all of which lead to a better social environment. Also important is teaching children how to manage and control impulses and how to manage anger, fear, stress, and frustration. It's equally important for students to learn communication skills, acceptance of responsibility, empathy, conflict resolution, and, above all, the give-and-take, "sharing is caring," and win-win principles. But this cannot be achieved without high-quality teachers who are equipped with knowledge of developmental psychology and social science.

Ultimately, quality teachers can be the catalyst in achieving a civilized and harmonious society—both locally and nationally. Teachers should be well trained in mentoring students and parents in the art of living together. To live together in harmony and survive without conflicts, focusing on the positives and advantages instead of the negatives and disadvantages is most important. Emotionally intelligent people, for example, avoid harsh criticism of others that embodies a destructive dynamic and can trigger a devastating feeling of hurt. Hurt feelings can trigger an adverse reaction and have a negative effect on motivation and interpersonal relationships. Hurt feelings usually sap one's energy and destroy confidence. Harsh and unconstructive criticism makes the receiving person feel unfairly attacked and resentful. It leads to demoralization and defensiveness, and ultimately the person becomes detached and isolated.

On the other hand, constructive and helpful criticism creates an effective atmosphere for cooperation and a harmonious working environment.

The above also applies to marriage, especially after the romance has faded and the intellectual conversation becomes mundane. At some point in marriage, partners start to take each other for granted. Respect diminishes, and accusations of stupidity and ignorance increase. Mutual devaluation escalates, and eventually life together becomes intolerable. What is the solution? Emotional intelligence that is reinforced by emotional literacy courses and counseling is an effective starting point. Accordingly, emotional intelligence classes should not be limited to school children. Social development requires the inclusion of adults and parents in emotional literacy.

Unfortunately, the standard school curriculum is deficient in teaching EI and SI. For the health and the prosperity of a nation, the emphasis on these subjects should be not less than the emphasis on literacy, science, and mathematics. A well-adjusted and balanced mind is more capable of comprehension than an anxious and depressed mind. Ignoring psychological literacy has a detrimental impact on the country's future. The prevalence of bullying, binge drinking, drug use, juvenile crime, and violence is a clear indication of the deficiency of the education system.

Quality Teachers

A good education system cannot be achieved without high-quality teachers with a master's degree in psychology and training in developmental psychology and emotional and social intelligences. Teachers must not only be qualified to teach, but they must also pass an emotional intelligence test in addition to literacy and numeracy tests. Teachers lacking emotional intelligence, literacy, and numeracy are not suitable to mentor children who need EI and SI development. Teachers should also have the capacity for critical thinking and logic, because when they are logical, they are able to apply logic in all situations. Individuals should be hired on the basis of interviews, demonstrated values and aptitude, and a written statement.

To attract better-quality university students to the teaching profession, schools with teaching programs should require higher entry marks, and employers should offer graduates an appropriate rate of pay. In addition, teachers should be assessed not only upon their entry into the university but upon graduation and after graduation as well.

After graduation, teachers should be provided with ongoing mentoring, training, and evaluation. Their evaluation and professional development should include regular classroom observations, coaching sessions, and feedback on the quality of their instruction. The system of review can break down teaching into some essentials, such as high standards for student achievement, quality and execution of lesson plans, and classroom culture. Following the periodic evaluation and training, the successful teacher's remuneration should be adjusted accordingly. Furthermore, the teaching profession should have a built-in motivation to excel.

It's understandable that someone who chooses to become a teacher is motivated by his or her passion for teaching; however, passion alone without material incentive can create a huge shortage of teachers. Such incentive is provided for doctors and engineers; without it, the world would be much worse off. A combination of passion, personal capacity, and material incentive in a profession are the key ingredients for any country that aspires to growth and progress. As it currently stands, many students become teachers as a last resort; because of their low marks, they are not accepted to study more rewarding courses. Only when society realizes the incredible importance of teachers and treats schools with the respect they deserve will the country have quality teachers—teachers who are not only passionate but highly qualified, inspired, and intelligent; teachers who have the knowledge and confidence to act as counselors, mentors, and support systems for the future generation.

To maintain high standards of an education system, school principals need to have the power of hiring and firing to ensure that only quality teachers are in the system and deadwood is kept out. This constitutes a major incentive for teachers to keep up-to-date and stay relevant. Here it should be emphasized that quality teachers can only be produced when their remuneration is appropriate to the task. As it stands, Western countries are aware of the problem but are not doing much about it. More unfortunate is that when the government attempts to improve the quality of teachers, some universities react as if their independence is under attack. Generally, universities are autonomous and self-governing institutions; they object, for example, if the government sets higher entry marks for those who wish to study teaching. In many countries, the entry marks for studying teaching (in at least three subjects including language) is 75 percent or lower, when it should be at least 85 percent. Attaining such an increase could be the best way to meet the standard required in the twenty-first century. Universities fear that increasing the entry marks will cause a drop in enrollment, which may have an impact on their viability. However, as discussed earlier, if the government increases the remuneration of teachers appropriate to their mission, the demand for enrollment will increase drastically.

Teachers who lay the foundation for future engineers shouldn't have lower entry marks to universities to study engineering. They also lay the foundation for the country's higher productivity by equipping the new generation with literacy and numeracy and helping students become balanced, well-adjusted, and emotionally and socially intelligent.

Quality teachers with expertise in human behavioral psychology should be well trained in the concept of the liberation of the human spirit. They should be able to become the most dynamic role models for their students. Quality teachers can focus students' attention on their emotional makeup, feelings, emotional literacy, social learning, and mental energy, without leaving any of the students out. Teachers cannot achieve results without being qualified in emotional literacy, effective motivation, prevention programs, and developmental psychology. Teachers should be equipped with knowledge on how society can take advantage of ethical values and individuals' capacities and how to achieve goals by exercising various avenues, such as foundational, quantitative, aesthetic, and logical methods that use students' intellect. At the same time—for reasons discussed earlier—these teachers can make it clear that having intelligence does not mean that one necessarily acts intelligently. There are many methodologies that teachers can use—relative to their observation of the students' perception—to help students understand various topics and promote problem solving by triggering the deep-thinking process.

Quality teachers should be able to bring self-awareness to students as well as the awareness of political and religious manipulation and deception. It's essential to know how and why religious leaders and politicians provoke feelings of cynicism and skepticism. Cynicism and skepticism are fully justified when politicians and religious leaders attempt to exploit the people's despair and insecurity by exaggerating issues. Teachers in this instance must be objective and free from personal ideological prejudice.

Quality teachers should be well inducted into social and political science on a bipartisan basis and should be equipped with a well-structured bipartisan curriculum. Accordingly, these teachers can point out that a nation controlled by money, self-serving politicians, dogmatic and ultraconservative religious leaders, and a right-wing media and press run by rich barons cannot be classified as free or democratically governed. Quality teachers can teach the true meaning of **_democracy_**, * which, under the current system of government, has lost its meaning.

> * **Democracy:** Western democracy, especially in the United States is being hijacked and manipulated by extreme capitalists who own the system and control the majority of politicians. It's extremely difficult for independent politicians to be elected without the sponsorship of vested interests and the media barons who constantly distort and mislead. They distort and mislead by targeting the less informed and the average voter with a barrage of propaganda campaigns. In the process, democracy loses its meaning, and citizens lose their faith in it. Money in politics can never lead to the necessary reforms. When wealth determines the degree of participation in the electoral process and when wealthy individuals and corporations have unlimited and undeclared spending on elections, democracy is doomed. The mutually reinforcing nature of economic injustice and political inequality are highlighted by election campaign financing, in which money is the king and the kingmaker, which is the path for the death of genuine democracy.

There is hope, however. And as mentioned earlier, it should come from adopting a moderate capitalist system and from instituting social and emotional education to produce better leaders and politicians. There is another hope that comes with the help of digital technology: people's attention is now diverted from the corrupt media, which for many decades was used for mind control. Fortunately, as can be witnessed in many countries, the digital revolution is starting to restore power to the people. Technology is empowering people to use their brains collectively to develop, express themselves, exchange information, and call for action at the stroke of a finger. Digital technology and social networking are allowing people to be informed and to choose for themselves. This technology is assisting the masses in collective solidarity without the guidance of the state and religion. However, people must be vigilant, as the vested interests have the capacity and the desire to corrupt whatever becomes detrimental to their survival.

Quality teachers should be able to instill in the young generation the value of the newly found freedom of expression and to ensure that everyone becomes vigilant in protecting what is lawfully theirs and defending true democracy. Quality teachers should also be able to fight any form of apathy in the young generation, because the apathy of one generation can destroy the hope and the future of the next.

Quality teachers can make it clear that in the absence of transparency, Western governments are elected and influenced by powerful lobbyist groups that represent only the vocal minority, the outcome of which is a corrupt government that serves the providers of capital for their election and the loud minority voices. It stands to reason that if a candidate is indebted to someone for funding his or her campaign, the candidate will follow instruction from and be loyal to the provider rather than to the people.

Ultimately, quality teachers are able to teach the principle stated by Socrates that knowing what ought to be done is one thing, and actually doing it is another. It is essential for teachers to think about how they can persuade more students to move from knowing what they ought to do to actually doing it. To achieve outcomes, quality teachers should not only be equipped with knowledge of behavioral science but with knowledge of creativity, inspiration, optimism, curiosity, and open-mindedness. They should be able to teach students to be proactive rather than reactive, to think win-win rather than win-lose, to understand first and then to be understood, and to begin with the end in mind to complete a plan. This is in addition to teaching students how to protect the environment and to live healthier, safer lives.

Racism and Discrimination

In civilized countries with progressive governments, legislation is in place to fight racism and other forms of discrimination. These legislations—essentially tools for encouraging empathy and tolerance—are helping to eradicate entrenched and institutionalized racism and discrimination. However, they are insufficient for eradicating the prejudice and bigotry that run through society. Prejudice and bigotry are the indirect and subconscious elements of racism and discrimination that can only be eradicated by education—starting in the early years of school. But education of children, on its own, will not resolve the problem. Schools need an accompanying program to include parents, who are generally one of the main causes of the problem. Changing parents' intellectual beliefs is easier than changing their attitudes.

In Western countries, despite many attempts to overcome the problem, racism and discrimination are still alive and well. The United States, for example, is a country that has been dominated by white people, and the rest have been treated like second-class citizens. Prejudice and bigotry is still directed toward Native Americans, African Americans, Muslim Americans, Asian Americans, Mexican Americans, Hispanic Americans, illegal immigrants, and other minority groups.

It is estimated that there are eleven million badly exploited illegal immigrants in the United States who have no legal or social protection. During economic growth, illegal immigrants, especially Mexicans (who constitute half of the United States' illegal immigrants) are allowed into the country to work for low wages, but they are hounded or deported during economic slowdowns. Illegal immigrants, whose cheap labor has for many decades helped build the US economy, are now being demonized. (The same occurred in some European countries, especially England and France, during their economic boom after World War II, when they allowed cheap labor from their colonies. Africans, Pakistanis, and Indians—all were treated like second-class citizens and are now despised).

Racial discrimination has occurred in employment, housing, and education, and it is even enacted by the government. US legislators recognized that people come to the United States for either money or freedom and decided to end formal racial discrimination. And so it was officially banned in the mid-twentieth century. Since then, racial discrimination has become socially unacceptable, except in racial politics, where it remains a major problem, especially in racist attitudes and prejudice against African Americans, illegal immigrants, Hispanics, and Muslims.

It should be noted, however, that following the resounding defeat of the Republican Party in the 2012 presidential election, some moderate Republicans decided to form a bipartisan group with the Democrats to resolve the immigrant issue. This could only happen when political, moral, and economic imperatives lined up, enabling Congress to move in the right direction to solve the long-standing humanitarian problem. The sad aspect of the story is that before discovering the political imperative, the Republicans had no concern for the moral imperative; it had no place in their theocratic establishment.

The other imperative worth mentioning here is the change of heart by the **Evangelicals,** * who once firmly opposed the acceptance and integration of Latinos. Their earlier opposition was part of a Catholic/Anglican sectarianism that they are now changing to embracement to bolster their power in areas where the Latinos live and congregate. In Frisco, Colorado, for example, the Latino population has increased by 70 percent over the last ten years, as immigrants have come looking for service-industry jobs. This population shift caused the Evangelical congregations to see the benefit of putting renewed emphasis on biblical commands to welcome strangers. They reached a radical change in their thinking, asking Congress to be more compassionate, when ten years earlier they were lobbying for tougher sanctions against undocumented Latino workers. Their own religious text of the New Testament says, "You must welcome the stranger and treat him as you would treat Jesus," and in Leviticus 19, "When a foreigner resides among you in your land, do not mistreat him." But unfortunately, when religion is mixed with politics, moral issues and imperatives can take on different interpretations. It can only be hoped that the Colorado experience can become the norm for antidiscrimination against the Latinos in other states where the Evangelicals are yet to be convinced, especially where the Latinos are in smaller numbers. As can be seen, society is dictated to by the imperatives of a hypocritical but vocal and powerful minority, while the silent majority is asleep.

* **Evangelicalism** is a worldwide Protestant historical movement that began in the 1730s at the time of emergence of the Methodists in England. The movement became significant in the United States during the Great

Awakenings of the eighteenth and nineteenth centuries. The United States has the largest concentration of Evangelicals, with roughly a quarter of the world's Evangelicals (over ninety million). The Evangelical faith is being born again, a shift based on passages in John (1:12–13 and 3:1–21) that call for a complete change of life. Their fundamental belief is in the apocalyptic end of times and the return of Christ. The central unifying ideology of their social movement is dominion over the secular institutions of the United States. Their survival largely depends on entangling religion with politics in order to enable the use of religion for lobbying purposes. They succeeded in converting the Republican Party into a nonsecular party of theocracy in which religion and politics are inseparable.

Discrimination and bigotry expose the United States' split personality in its constitutional and cultural aspects, which means that the First Amendment of the US Constitution has lost its meaning. This is especially evident when one looks at the Republican Party, which is dominated by the extreme religious Right groups in the Tea Party. It's a party that is in turn dominated by the Evangelicals, who have a stranglehold on the Republican Party. The irony is that the Evangelicals were for many years in total opposition to allowing Latinos a path to citizenship. Their change of heart came about when they reached the conclusion that the Republicans would never control the White House without the Latinos' votes, which are overwhelmingly directed to the Democrats. The Evangelicals' attitude could have resulted from the fact that the majority of Latinos are Catholics, but in politics and religion, there is no moral imperative, only manipulation, deception, and hypocrisy.

The extreme Right groups don't understand that racism and discrimination create a demoralized, underprivileged class, which results in resentment and eventual social upheaval. They also don't understand that demoralized people become less productive and less responsive to team spirit. The country's technological advances depend on well-coordinated skills to produce a positive outcome. Making disturbance of harmony within a work group is detrimental to the productivity of any organization and, ultimately, the country. It is more so when racism and discrimination are directed against ethnic or religious minorities that constitute a sizable proportion of the population and the workforce. The success of any country depends on the opportunity given to its entire people to develop, flourish, and reach their potential and individuality. In return, if they are treated as equals, they develop the feeling of belonging and patriotism, which no country in the world can afford to lose. Tolerance of others, inclusiveness, and fairness must be the guiding principles of any nation. A united nation is strong and prosperous, and a divided nation is always in decline. A leader who promotes disunity for the sake of his or her political or religious survival is unpatriotic and acting against the national interests.

The disgraceful behavior of some bigoted religious and political leaders in their attempts to marginalize some sectors of their community is causing resentment and revolt. Being subjected to unwarranted humiliation motivates minority groups to fight for dignity and survival, which benefits no one but leads to the fragmentation of society. Prejudice and bigotry are against the civil rights of every citizen under the Constitution that was meant to promote equality and ethical human relations. Discrimination on the grounds of race, religion, ethnic origin, gender, and physical disability causes resentment and brings out the worst in people. Any government or group that engages in racial and ethnic discrimination through employment, housing, or education, especially against economically disadvantaged social groups, should be condemned. It stands to reason that if all religious and political leaders are enlightened and united on the subject of equality, society will be harmonious and prosperous. This applies to any country with a population from various racial, religious, ethnic, and social backgrounds.

There is a strong element of casual racism in the world despite the adoption of antiracism policies. Of course, adopting a policy is different from backing the policy with a sustained program for eliminating the underlying roots of the problem. One such program should be the introduction of school curricula commencing at preschool and continuing to the university level, complete with assessment and exams. All programs should be based on the agreed principles adopted by the International Convention on the Rights of the Child. All programs should be backed up by a zero-tolerance approach to racial abuse and vilification. Entrenched bigotry and discrimination emanate from humans' primitive mistrust and jealousy of those who don't belong to the family or the tribe. Historically, this was one of the main causes of many conflicts, wars, massacres, and genocides. To eliminate the problem, it is necessary to start by fighting its elementary, primitive causes, which is not an easy task. It requires a good investment in everything possible to bring society to a real civilized status. Civilization was able to modify many negative human instincts; bigotry is one of those negative instincts that still must be fought.

It must be emphasized that a united and happy workforce has the advantage of creativity and diversity, which is the strength of any highly productive organization. The outcome of a demoralized and disharmonious workforce is the complete opposite. Furthermore, people who are affected by **harassment**, ** racism, and discrimination often react with violence. In any community, if some members are left behind with nothing left to lose, an unpleasant outcome should be expected. Only through secular education and experience can people get rid of bigotry and develop common sense, positive spontaneity, free thinking, creativity, and free spirit without political and religious divisiveness and irrationality. It is appropriate here to emphasize that good citizenship occurs when people accept each other and reject discrimination. And a good politician is one who promotes equality, individuality, diversity, and fair-go principles. Through a well-structured secular education system, people can develop a new generation of nation builders equipped with wisdom based on common sense, rational thinking, and objectivity.

** **Harassment** is the term that covers different types of offensive behaviors that are intended to disturb or threaten others. These behaviors are generally repetitive, abusive, and unwanted. Harassment can be psychological, racial, religious, or sexual. It is inflicted on victims by humiliation or intimidation and by targeting individuals because of their race, ethnicity, religion, or sexual orientation.*

School Dropouts

The education system in the United States and in many other so-called civilized countries is producing many dropouts due to a lack of prevention programs in mentoring relationships, as well as the lack of government funding, especially in the highest-need public schools. Here it should be emphasized that many Western countries are still living in the past, when the family was a solid unit and religions were strong enough to enforce principles of obedience, conformity, and morality. Today, however, the family as a concept has begun to disintegrate, individuality is becoming the basis of the social structure, and religion is being abandoned due to its divisiveness, hypocrisy, contradictions, and dogmatic idealism. This leaves the schools to serve as a social armor, especially for kids from low-income backgrounds, abandoned kids, and others who are taken away from their families due to domestic violence or an unsuitable living environment.

Unfortunately, governments, instead of increasing funding for schools—especially public and disadvantaged schools—are reducing it. More funds, instead, are going to wealthy religious and advantaged schools that can already afford quality education, depriving the majority of poor and desperate ones. In the process, the hidden talent, potential, and untapped brilliance of many poor kids fall by the wayside, to the detriment of the country's survival and prosperity. The consequence of inequality in education is a great number of school dropouts.

More must be done to reduce the dropout rate, especially at the high school level. Currently there is no thorough research into the impact of students' transitional stage from the secondary level into high school, though a major nurturing and psychological adjustment at this age is necessary. As it stands, the school systems are not geared to pay attention to the problem, nor are enough human and financial resources allocated to deal with it. To identify students showing warning signs in behavior and performance, additional qualified counselors and social workers need to be involved in the school structure. This will allow schools' administrations to allocate appropriate resources for improving outcomes. It will also help schools to encourage parents' participation in problem solving.

In pursuit of better schools, many researchers suggest the need for a major correction of the way funding is distributed. Because of the religious industry's influence on and control over politicians, Western countries are subsidizing private and religious schools at the expense of public and disadvantaged schools. As a consequence, the poor and disadvantaged schools produce less-fortunate youth that become unemployable and, in some instances, antisocial and criminal.

It is common that the funding system generates large differences between wealthy and impoverished groups. Private and religious schools in different countries are subsidized by taxpayers' money by different methods that are in addition to the high fees paid to schools by the wealthy parents (parents who, in many instances, claim the incurred cost against their income in their tax returns). In addition, wealthy parents use many loopholes to minimize their taxes when the rest of the population doesn't have the resources or the knowledge to do so. The wealthy also have the resources to hire private tutors, which will always give their children an educational advantage. Above all, the wealthy can nourish their children much better than the poor can nourish theirs, and nourishment is an essential element for the brain's proper development and functioning. No matter what, there will always be advantages and distinction for the rich over the poor, and this is acceptable in a capitalist system, provided that the adopted capitalist system is moderate, with a fair distribution of wealth. (For a discussion of the impact of extreme capitalism, see chapter 3.)

In some countries, subsidy is provided by vouchers or tax credit; in other countries, all schools receive equal-per-student funding from general tax revenues. In all cases, private and religious schools are given the privilege of siphoning desperately needed funds from the public school system without offering the equal access that is the hallmark of public education.

In the United States, for example, the education funds in some states are diverted to the private and religious schools through the use of tuition vouchers. This system allows prosperous families the opportunity to pursue further prosperity for their children, which degrades public education. Some other states with a similar impact on public education allow the use of scholarship tax credits, through which the states provide education savings accounts that allow public money to be used for tuition, stationeries, and books. The worst part of this arrangement is the 2002 US Supreme Court ruling that stated that providing school vouchers—which can be used at religious schools—doesn't violate the separation of church and state. This is despite the fact that such use of vouchers contradicts the principle of the right of every child to have a good public education. When religious and private school tuition is a taxpayer expense, many US students do not get the education they deserve, especially in high-poverty schools at the lower grades. It's a discriminatory practice to make one section of the community succeed by leaving the rest behind, and this is what extreme capitalism is doing to the so-called richest and most powerful nation in the world, where good education is provided, depending on where the students live.

Depriving public and disadvantaged schools proper funding makes the religious schools more attractive to wealthy parents. In the process, religion triumphs over secularism and conformism over individualism; as a result, the kids are exposed to brainwashing. Ultimately, the country ends up inhibiting children's creativity and enlightenment, especially by promoting creationism over science.

At the heart of the problem is the violation of the secular system of government, in which the church and state are to be separate. How, for example, can a country and students benefit from religious teachings such as what Jesus said in Matthew 22:37: "Love the Lord your God with all your heart, soul, and mind?" How can this and other religious teachings contribute to students' deep thinking and scientific education? (For more on indoctrination, see my earlier books, *Israel vs. America vs. the World* and *Death by Choice versus Religious Dogma.*)

It's worth noting that religious schools represent 85 percent of the total private school enrollment in most Western countries. The religious schools by their nature combine **proselytization*** with education and therefore should not be funded by taxpayer dollars, especially when the public school system—unlike the selective religious school system—is open to all citizens. Public schools are compelled to accept and educate all students, including those from diverse backgrounds, learning levels, and abilities. Religious and private schools, on the other hand, are allowed to pick and choose which students they admit. Furthermore, religious schools are not required to comply with the country's civil rights laws and can exclude students based on their religion, gender, or mental or physical disabilities.

***Proselytization** is the attempt to make or convert one to a religion or a cause.*

The key to any country's progress and prosperity depends largely on the strength of its education system. Here it should be emphasized that to minimize dropouts, especially at the high school level, there should be thorough research carried out into the impact of students' transitional stage from secondary school into high school, the time when a major psychological adjustment is necessary.

Another key issue is the unaffordable college education for the poor, which is causing more students' dropouts because of the high fees.

Religion's Impact on Psychology

To avoid the indoctrination of children, it may be necessary to expose them to a variety of ideologies and beliefs of a secular and nonsecular nature that can stimulate their thinking and help them to reason rationally. Children should also be mentally equipped with a wide horizon of knowledge to enable them to make appropriate judgments about many aspects of life. Parents should make every effort to protect their children from any form of brainwashing and indoctrination if they want their children to grow to be normal, reasonable, creative, uninhibited, and freethinking.

It's worth mentioning here Albert Einstein's description of belief in God. In a letter dated January 3, 1954, written to the philosopher Eric Gutkind, he called it "childish superstition." He added, "The word God is for me nothing more than the expression and product of human weaknesses, the Bible a collection of honorable, but still primitive legends, which are nevertheless pretty childish. No interpretation no matter how subtle can (for me) change this." Einstein's previous comments on religion, such as, "Science without religion is lame, religion without science is blind," were subject to a great debate, used mainly to back up arguments in favor of religion.

It is understandable why Einstein made his negative description of belief in God. It is simply because religion is the opposite of science. And because science is founded on doubt and deals with realities, tested theories, verifiable information, and facts, while religion is founded on absolutism, subjective ideology, speculation, mysteries, and metaphors about God.

Through secular education and experience, students can avoid religious subjectivity and sectarianism, which embody bigotry and prejudice. Good citizenship occurs when people accept one another and reject discrimination. A good secular politician is one who constantly promotes equality, individuality, diversity and fair-go principles. Civilized countries are mature enough to develop a secular school curriculum for teaching logic, rational thinking, common sense, and associated subjects in order to develop a new generation of nation builders equipped with wisdom and objectivity. Highly educated and motivated nations can, through free education, produce brilliant people, the prime movers of their countries. They become the source of the innovations, discoveries, growth, and development that secure their countries' future. Unfortunately, some governments ignore the fact that when education is unaffordable to half of the population, many brilliant brains stay dormant and undiscovered. It must be remembered that free education is essential for high productivity and prosperity.

Furthermore, critical messages can be objectively explained by good teachers in public schools and not in religious schools. For example, in public schools, teachers can explain that human interference with the carbon and nitrogen cycles is having a devastating effect on the planet and is the cause of climate change and global warming. Overpopulation increases the need for urbanization and the demand for energy, especially fossil fuels. Religious schools, on the other hand, are incapable of teaching students the danger of increasing the population in our fragile environment because such teachings are in conflict with what God said to Adam—"go forth and multiply"—and disrupt the competition between religious groups such as Muslims and Christians to increase their constituencies and power bases. All of this and the religious dogma of "God gives life and God takes it away" as well as the continuous campaign against birth control and abortions disqualify religious schools as objective institutions. This is one of the negative outcomes society gets when religious education is subsidized by taxpayer money. Religious leaders' advocacy and action against birth control and abortions is resulting in the divergence from the law of "maintenance of the balance of nature," which normally applies to other species. Religious doctrines have no regard to the exponential growth of population, which is combined with the

Industrial Revolution that tipped the balance against the environment.

Religious leaders through religious schools employ mass psychology as one of their methods of indoctrinating children to achieve conformism and **obedience.** * The average person's susceptibility to mind control and tendency toward herding behavior are the principal human weaknesses these leaders exploit in order to meet their objectives. Furthermore, the overzealous ones choose only emotional and manageable issues, ignoring the inconvenient issues that have the potential to lead individuals to self-awareness. By cherry-picking issues, such as legalization of euthanasia and abortion, and using emotive phrases like "sanctity of life," they scare the hell out of politicians to deter them from making legitimate social decisions, in fear of religious backlash. Politicians usually respond to a vocal minority rather than a silent majority. The truth is that over 70 percent of religious people and over 80 percent of the populations in Western countries are in favor of euthanasia and abortion legalization.

> * **Obedience** is used here in the context of indoctrination and not in terms of discipline. Many parents send their children to religious schools because of a misconception about achieving better outcomes from discipline. Obedience and regimentation in religious terms are part of mind control, which results in children losing

their creativity by conforming to religious dogmas and religious interests and leads to the herd mentality. Losing creativity usually leads to a diminished capacity for innovation and free spirit, which no country in the world can afford to ignore. Obedience doesn't help the independence and individuality of children, nor does it help their freethinking. Most likely it causes children to grow up with inhibitions. (Obedient and regimented children do what they're told and don't think for themselves.) St. Paul in the New Testament said, "Slaves be obedient to your masters."

Parents also need to be reminded that sending children to some historically known religious establishments and schools where the practice of pedophilia is common could be a recipe for disaster. It is the parents' responsibility not to bury their heads in the sand through blind trust and devotion to religious beliefs. Parents by now should know that their responsibility to protect their children is well overdue. Parents who send their children to these religious places should know that leaders of these religious organizations have always covered up and avoided legal penalties. For how long were parents hearing about the leaders of these organizations, their continuous qualified apologies, and occasional compensations to their victims? How much evidence do parents need to revolt against organizations that have caused so much heartache and so many suicides of innocent victims?

These problems are in addition to the design of religious education, which limits the acquisition and the acceptance of general and scientific knowledge to prevent people from reaching different conclusions from those of dogmatic religious teachings. Religion, being based on conjecture, is comprehensible only to people who believe in it blindly, especially the ones who are indoctrinated early in life. Secularly educated and self-aware people are the biggest hurdle confronting these leaders because they are less susceptible to emotional blackmail, and at the same time, they become the source for development of others. Knowledge and emotional intelligence are the necessary ingredients for conscious reasoning to counter the effect of the targeting of emotions. Religious leaders, by virtue of their social intelligence, are well aware of human weaknesses and capable of employing many methods for trapping the unwary, especially children.

In the process of indoctrination, the seeds sown by subjective religious leaders for the power and glory of their sects are often the cause of conflicts. Many people have been killed in the name of religion. Religion is meant to give people peace and harmony, but unfortunately, it leads to conflicts and wars. Religious extremism and the current rise of religious fundamentalism are generated by religious leaders in their quest for influence and control. Generally, conflict is caused by religious indoctrination and the creation of blind followers who become part of subjective sectarianism. Indoctrination of followers is the result of competition between Jews, Christians, and Muslims and the many sects within. Competition is the result of religion being a commercial enterprise, run by vested interests. Conflicts will continue to fester while there are enough blind believers willing to follow manipulative and ambitious religious leaders. Fortunately, however, members of the younger generation are becoming more educated and more closely associated with scientific progress than their parents were, which is causing religious influence to diminish. The slide in religious entrenchment can be easily observed by comparing religion's present influence with that of the past, when ignorance and illiteracy were widespread. Religion is diminishing, despite constant attempts (to remain profitable) to reinvent it to make it acceptable to people.

In my book *Israel vs. America vs. the World*, (2011), I wrote:

> Blind commitment and total loyalty to a religious faith or ethnic nationalism often leads to antipathy and prejudice, and sometimes hatred toward others. Furthermore, when prejudices are formed in early childhood, their eradication becomes a major psychological problem. However, since bigotry and prejudice are originally learned psychological complexes, counterlearning in a well-structured school curriculum designed for developing emotional intelligence can help to eradicate the problem.

The religious enterprise has promoted myths as absolute truth and has been able to convince people that the only path to heaven is through religion. Through peddling myths, religious leaders were able to build huge empires with huge wealth, while telling their followers to reject a materialistic way of living. To maintain their power and control and build huge empires, they divided people by promoting prejudice, bigotry, and subjectivity. They promoted the ***fear of God***** and the promise of the afterlife as tools to control human emotions, especially the feeling of guilt, which requires constant confessions and repentance, followed by constant donations to the religious empires. Using the power of their empires, they were able to control politicians to ensure that religious schools would be subsidized by taxpayers, achieving a negative outcome for the nation in allowing backwardness to fester. Fortunately, through scientific progress and secular education, people are gradually becoming more aware of their physical world and the empirical evidence. The younger generation is now more enlightened and equipped to reject the mysticism, superstition, and metaphysics that are the domain of religions.

** ***Fear of God*** *is fear of the unknown, fear of the final judgment, and fear of going to hell. These tools have been used by the religious industry for many centuries to control human emotions and behaviors.*

Despite the above statements about religion, my intention here is not to change the world drastically but to get rid of fear, guilt, indoctrination, and the manipulation of humans' herding instinct. I wish to eliminate all the negatives of mind control that inhibit people's creativity and individuality. It is not possible to completely eradicate religious influence while the world is in a transitional stage, an evolutionary process of shifting from the entrenched dogmatic beliefs into the futuristic scientific age. It could take another two hundred years for science and logic to totally eclipse religious fairy tales. However, it is possible to eradicate religious control over politicians by shedding the apathy and raising the awareness of the majority.

Religions still have a role to play when illiteracy and ignorance in many countries are still rife. A start, however, is now overdue for enlightened countries to begin shedding rigid, outdated religious idealism and conflict-creating philosophies. It's unfortunate that only a few moderate religious leaders are emerging to influence the modernization of religions to meet the needs of the twenty-first century and beyond, especially to ensure the continuity of social and moral stability in the transitional period. Moderate leaders, especially the ones with openness to science are essential for curbing the control of ultraconservative and fundamentalist religious leaders over the political agenda. Ultraconservative and fundamentalist religious leaders are not only backward looking, but they also strive to divide the people of the world by sectarianism. Their stubborn refusal to shift ground on many critical social and scientific issues is causing religion to be discounted as a source for human comfort and progress.

To avoid religious subjectivity and the conflict it creates, people are finding alternative and more realistic sources. Today, social progress and sophistication can be measured by people's attitudes toward science, technology, women's rights, and the adoption of a secular system of government and secular social culture. On the other hand, backwardness can be measured by the dominance of religion on people's daily lives, the adoption of a nonsecular system of government, belief in life after death, belief in miracles, and the widespread belief in superstitions. Above all is the prevalence of myths and mysticism in cultural life. In backward societies, myths and religion have a role to play in giving comfort to the weak and the less-informed members of the community who live on hope and the belief that the next life will be better. In these societies, religious leaders use theatrical and euphoric ceremonies and mystical participation rituals designed to create an atmosphere for fusion of groups to make them susceptible to mass conditioning and mind control. These methods, used over many centuries to entrench religious beliefs, have become an essential part of many cultures and traditions.

In my book *Death by Choice vs. Religious Dogma*, (2012), I wrote,

> Religion traps people in the box of subjectivity at an early age. This makes it difficult for the less-informed people to become free thinkers. Setting oneself free from something one didn't choose in the first place

requires deep thinking. It is ultimately the individual's knowledge, self-analysis, and critical thinking that can get him or her out of the box and to freedom...

To achieve their objectives, religious leaders employ mass psychology and brainwashing techniques on their constituency. They indoctrinate children early, when they are most susceptible...

The indoctrination of children is a form of abuse. Secular society should never sacrifice its most valuable assets to the religious industry. It is ridiculous that some of the so-called civilized countries so heavily subsidize religious schools for such a negative outcome: the triumph of conformity over individuality, which retards children's creativity and produces the herd mentality, benefiting the religious industry at the expense of society...

Religious leaders, for their own survival, achieve their objectives by entangling religion with politics to allow themselves to use religion for lobbying purposes. In the process, they render the secular system of government and democracy meaningless...

Through their subjective and manipulative interpretation of the scripture, they instill in people's minds that their brand of religion is the only truth, despite the ideological truth's being relative. (The ideological truth can be one thing to one person and the opposite to others.) In the process, they create sects, religious intolerance, and conflicts. The ultimate outcome, as we have witnessed, is sectarian fragmentation of the world.

As it stands, enlightened people have evolved to have emotional intelligence, to distinguish the good from the bad, to believe in social justice, and to see that high moral values are no longer the monopoly of religion.

Finally, psychologist Peter Salovey, in regard to the future of emotional intelligence, (1990), said, "I think in the coming decade we will see well-conducted research demonstrating that emotional skills and competencies predict positive outcomes at home with one's family, in school, and at work. The real challenge is to show that emotional intelligence matters over-and-above psychological constructs that have been measured for decades, like personality and IQ. I believe that emotional intelligence holds this promise."

CHAPTER 3

Social Intelligence

Definition

Social intelligence is sophisticated information processing adapted to the social domain. It is natural and relates to the survival instinct and the survival of a species. It is advanced in humans, who are social animals. It is present in other animals, especially monkeys that live within a hierarchical system, but it is most sophisticated in humans due to the capacity of their social brain. Still, the degree of sophistication depends largely on an individual's IQ and emotional intelligence; the higher these two intelligences, the higher one's degree of social intelligence.

Evolutionary psychologists suggest that the social brain, or social intelligence, evolved to meet the challenges of navigating the social currents in a primate group, such as determining who the superior is, who can be depended on, and who the others must please and follow. In humans, the additional need for social engagement, coordination, cooperation, and competition contributed to brain development. The major social functions of the human brain became the capacity for interaction, empathy, learning, and concern for others.

The ingredients of social intelligence, as broadly expressed by Daniel Goleman in his book, *Social Intelligence*, (2007), are social awareness (what we sense about others) and social facility (what we do with that awareness). This includes feeling with others, listening and attuning to a person, and knowing how the social world works, which includes everything that leads to positive and effective interaction with others.

In the same book, Goleman discusses the digital revolution and the resultant social phenomenon that is causing the new generation to disconnect. Modern technologies such as iPods, Facebook, and Twitter are diminishing the bonding, face-to-face contact, and interpersonal relationships that are the foundation of social interaction and factors that have a profound influence on mood and brain chemistry. Mood and brain chemistry require us to be socially responsive and wise. According to Goleman, "Wisdom can hardly develop without direct human connectivity or while an iPod is plugged into our ears. He observes that the technological revolution has had a negative impact on human relations and has caused the generation gap to widen."

Goleman, however, doesn't take into consideration the following:

- First, this has always been the case following the adoption of new technologies since the Industrial Revolution. Perhaps social intelligence is not diminishing but is taking on a new form and different dimensions.

- Second, the younger generation has an advantage over the older generation in the efficient use of technology that leads to higher productivity and provides access to vast sources of information on mobile devices and the Internet. As more people gain access to the Internet, the world's population becomes increasingly connected and empowered; people have more choices and are able to share more information. Generally, indications point to major improvements in health and economic outcomes for any nation that embraces modern technology.

Furthermore, connectivity and empowerment of youth is increasing—as was observed in Egypt during the so-called Arab Spring, which should be called the Arab Nightmare following the military coup. The new military dictatorship will be unsustainable, especially when poverty, high unemployment rates, and food and energy inflation exist, and the majority has nothing else left to lose. The survival of bad leaders will be short-lived, especially if the outcome is more economic stagnation and high unemployment among the youth. The connectivity and the empowerment of the youth will most likely create havoc and cause the toppling of any corrupt government and any unjust system. (For more on the turmoil in the Middle East and North Africa, see chapter 5 of my book *Israel vs. America vs. the World*.)

- Third, the wisdom of the younger generation will come from consciousness about the natural environment and its protection. Previous generations, because of lack of wisdom, caused great damage to the environment, which the younger generation has inherited. The new generation is grappling with global warming, climate change, and pollution, all of which will take many decades to repair. Worse yet, the most-needed repairs of the environment are currently hampered by vested interests and skeptics of the ruling older generation.

- Ultimately, the younger generation has a much bigger responsibility to act collectively with greater social intelligence to deal with the many problems that the older generations have left behind. Solving these problems will require social and scientific approaches that involve multiple skills and teamwork. Their success depends largely on their disposition for collaboration and interpersonal relations. Accordingly, the new generation must learn that connectivity and social intelligence are more than an iPod plugged into an ear. Of course, they still have to breed through face-to-face contact using their moods and brain chemistry.

Essentially, social intelligence can be defined as the art of relating to people, which consists of the qualities of charisma and leadership. It's the ability to connect with others;

it's about making others feel better and more productive and more positive. It's also about guiding people's thoughts and perceptions. Finally, social intelligence implies social integrity and keeping true to one's own feelings, the opposite of **social pretension.***

* Social pretension relates to one's public face that contradicts his or her private reality. Often, social pretenders don't do what they say, especially when they say things just to impress. They are obsessed with impression management to achieve their objectives. This phenomenon is common in politicians, religious leaders, actors, salespeople, lawyers, and some narcissists.

(For more on charisma and leadership, see subheadings below, and for more on pretension, see the discussion of narcissism in chapter 5.)

The development of our modern understanding of social intelligence dates back to the early twentieth century:

- In the 1920s and 1930s, Edward Thorndike** described social intelligence as the ability to get along with other people. Many of his early studies focused on describing, defining, and assessing socially competent behavior.

- In the forties, David Wechsler*** suggested that affective components of intelligence may be essential to success in life. He defined intelligence as the aggregate or global capacity of the individual to act purposefully, to think rationally, and to deal effectively with his or her environment. His line of research helped define human effectiveness from the social perspective and strengthened his definition of general intelligence, which he revised in 1958 to include, "the capacity of the individual to act purposefully."

- In the nineties, theorists like Peter Salovey and John Mayer viewed emotional intelligence as part of social intelligence. They suggested that not only were the two concepts related, but that they were likely interrelated components of the same construct.

- Since 2000, scholars have begun to shift their attention from describing and assessing social intelligence to understanding the purpose of interpersonal behavior and the role it plays in effective adaptability. A modern person with emotional intelligence can easily understand how interaction with others works and can easily develop social intelligence, especially in understanding the impact of modern technologies, such as mobile communication systems, social media, and the Internet, on human relationships.

** *Edward Thorndike* (1874–1949) was an American psychologist who spent nearly his entire career at Teachers College, Columbia University.

He graduated from The Roxbury Latin School (1891) in West Roxbury, Massachusetts, and from Wesleyan University (BS 1895). He earned an MA at Harvard University in 1897. His work on animal behavior and the learning process led to the theory of connectionism and helped lay the scientific foundation for modern educational psychology. He also worked on solving industrial problems, such as employee exams and testing. He was a member of the board of the Psychological Corporation and served as president of the American Psychological Association in 1912.

*** **David Wechsler** (1896–1981) was a leading American psychologist. He developed well-known intelligence scales, such as the Wechsler Adult Intelligence Scale (WAIS) and the Wechsler Intelligence Scale for Children (WISC). He was born in Romania and immigrated with his parents to the United States as a child. He studied at the City College of New York and Columbia University, where he earned his master's degree in 1917 and his PhD in 1925. He became chief psychologist at Bellevue Psychiatric Hospital in 1932, where he stayed until 1967. He is best known for his intelligence tests. He was one of the most influential advocates of the role of nonintellective factors in testing. He emphasized that factors other than intellectual ability are involved in intelligent behavior. He objected to the single score offered by the 1937 Binet scale. Although his test did not directly measure nonintellective factors, it took these factors into careful account in its underlying theory. He assigned an arbitrary value of one hundred to the mean intelligence and added or subtracted another fifteen points for each standard deviation above or below the mean where the subject was. He divided the concept of intelligence into two main areas: verbal and performance (non-verbal) scales, each evaluated with different subtests.

It's worth returning back to Daniel Goleman and his book, *Social Intelligence*, (2007), in which he describes a social model of intelligence drawn from the emerging field of social neuroscience. He demonstrates how relationships have the power to shape human experiences and neurobiological perspectives, such as sexual attraction, marriage, parenting, psychopathic behaviors, and group relationships. He describes the power of social interaction to influence mood and brain chemistry, attachment, bonding, and the making and remaking of memory as he examines how our brains are wired for altruism, compassion, concern, and rapport. He discusses the human ability to manage emotions for positive relationships and the ability to connect with one another on the basis that humans are wired to connect.

Goleman also divides social intelligence into social awareness and social facility. The social awareness category consists of primal empathy, ***attunement***, ** empathic accuracy, and social cognition. The social facility category consists of synchrony, self-presentation, influence, and concern. These categories are all about understanding others' feelings, thoughts, and intentions to allow effective interactions.

** ***Attunement*** *is attention that goes beyond momentary empathy to a full, sustained presence that facilitates rapport by real listening, reciprocal dialogue, and mutual understanding.*

It should be noted that, according to Goleman, research-ers into neuroscience have recently discovered biological, chemical, and structural aspects of the brain that cor-respond to fluency in social interactions. When people strongly connect in social situations, the chemical activ-ity in each person's brain actually syncs with that of the other participants. This causes a ripple effect throughout the body, causing greater and greater physiological con-nections. A person with high social intelligence has this effect to a much greater degree than others. A charismatic person, for example, can affect the physiology of a crowd of hundreds or even thousands. Such research, Goleman claims, will have a profound effect on the theory of social interactions and interpersonal relationships. Goleman also explains "the capacity for joy" and how it affects our social intelligence. He shows how our resilience plays an impor-tant role in our happiness, which comes into play as we express ourselves to others.

Human relations stem from genetic and environmental factors. Genetics refers to the biological systems that regu-late human emotions, and, as discussed in the following chapter, environmental factors are based on knowledge and experience.

Human feelings and our ability during interaction to make each other happy or aggravated, or to feel better or worse are transmitted by signals to the brain and biology. It's the repeated and the reverse signals that affect our interactions and experiences. Emotions are contagious; we transmit our moods to others when we are happy or miserable. We can make others feel good or unhappy. Through social interaction and exchange of emotions—positive and negative—we transfer our feelings by a smile or by an angry face that makes the other person happy, sad, fearful, or revengeful. Social interaction transmits our emotions to others and others' emotions to us. This spread of feelings to someone else is a natural phenomenon that happens with every human encounter. Emotion can pass from person to person silently, without being consciously noticed.

Personality

Personality, by definition, consists of intelligence, emotional intelligence, and social intelligence, as discussed earlier, and wisdom as discussed in the next chapter.

Personality is one's enduring patterns of thought, feeling, and behavior, and it is usually unique in each individual, reflected in the person's actions and reactions in different circumstances. Other than the inherited components of personality, one's response to reward and punishment and other behaviors, such as impulse control and drive, depend largely on learning.

A critical element of understanding personality is the ability to understand how conditioning, individualism, conformism, and the use of mass psychology work. Having a basic understanding of psychology and the sources and components of personality could be a necessary step toward countering the effects of mass psychology, manipulation, and indoctrination, which are the forces behind distorted human relations and the reason for constant human conflict, prejudice, and bigotry. This understanding, which embodies the development of emotional and social intelligences, is the catalyst for better communication between people. It also leads to developing an individual's capacity to resolve most common personality disorders, such as unhealthy narcissism, insecurity, and inferiority complex. Understanding common human behaviors and aspirations is the pathway to social harmony and to a better conflict-resolution process between people.

One of the main advantages of understanding one's psychology, which embodies self-analysis and self-awareness, is the ridding oneself of the constant projection of a false image that is caused by insecurity or the feeling of inferiority, which in turn leads to unhealthy narcissism. (For more on insecurity, inferiority, and narcissism, see chapter 5.)

Describing other aspects of intelligence and emotional intelligence that relate to the formation of personality, I wrote the following in *Thorny Opinion*, (2008):

> There are inherent and environmental factors that contribute to the development of our personality that can be defined by highlighting the main sources as follows:
>
> - heredity
> - environment (social and natural)
>
> Social psychologists are generally divided on the degree of influence of each of these sources on the

formation of personality, but it could be assumed to be equal. However, currently, there are various genetic studies around the world that will lead to further clarification in the near future.

Heredity relates to the genetic makeup of a person, which is the result of the transmission of genes through the chromosome from one generation to another. It is the outcome of instinctive natural selection, which results in different biological and behavioral characteristics in different people. Intelligence and temperament are prominent characteristics, partially transmitted between generations by heredity and partially assisted by interaction with the environment.

Science is now trying to influence the characteristics' outcome through genetic manipulation. The ethical dilemma of altering human genetic makeup, however, is restricting the intensive research needed to interfere with the natural selection criteria.

Environment (social and natural) relates to all aspects of a person's environment, including natural, social, physical, philosophical, psychological, and cultural aspects and encompasses all the learning and observations that have contributed to an individual's development since birth. These variables could result in different behavioral outcomes in different people…

Motivation for example, could vary in many different ways, both at home and at school, and may have a different impact, relative to each child's perception.

Personality formation starts early in childhood, beginning when parents apply methods to influence their children's behavior, which could differ in accordance with their children's methods of attracting the parents' attention…

When the parents respond to the need or the demand of the child as a result of a scream or a tantrum (not to be confused with the natural need for the child to scream), the child might adopt the same method again and again. Barring no other countering influences, the child could develop into an aggressive and forceful person. On the other hand, if the parents respond to the child's need in a timely and disciplined manner, smiling, happy, and affectionate, the child might develop into a placid, amiable, and compassionate person. Therefore, the child's behavior largely depends on the parents' usual response, which contributes to the conditioning and the development of the child's personality.

Charisma

The classical religious definition of charisma is, "A certain quality of an individual's personality by virtue of which he or she is set apart from ordinary men and women and treated as endowed with supernatural, superhuman, or at least specifically exceptional powers or qualities. These are such as are not accessible to the ordinary person but are regarded as of divine origin or as exemplary, and on the basis of them, the individual concerned is treated as a leader. It's the followers that endow the individual with powers, regard these powers, and treat him or her as a leader. Charisma can only be that which believers recognize as charismatic in those they treat as such."

In Christianity, a charismatic person is one who is divinely bestowed with power or talent. Christianity assumes charisma cannot be acquired but is rather a divine gift. Charisma refers especially to a quality in certain people who easily draw the attention and admiration—or even hatred, if the application of such charisma is perceived to be negative—of others. Unfortunately, throughout religious history, it is mostly hatred and conflicts that religious charismatic leaders have achieved. Charisma was also used negatively by sinister political leaders such as Hitler and Stalin.

While the origin and original usage of the word *charisma* imply Christian religious connections, the concept of charisma as God-given has become largely obsolete, except among totally devoted and dogmatic religious people. The notion that charismatic qualities are inborn is not easy to substantiate. There are many examples of people who develop charisma through training and experience, just as there are many people who develop qualities of leadership.

Another definition of a charismatic person is one who stands out in the crowd—one with positive energy, an aura of captivation, and the ability to connect with, change, and motivate people.

Charisma by itself is no guarantee of effective leadership, but charisma tends to result from effective leadership and the qualities that enable effective leadership. It's common for a charismatic leader to have extensive knowledge of the social environment and philosophy, to be skilled in public speaking, and to possess high levels of emotional and social intelligences. A charismatic person has a special personal quality or power that makes him or her capable of influencing or inspiring large numbers of people with enthusiasm and devotion. It is the person with high social intelligence who can affect the physiology of a crowd. Charisma is closely related to assertiveness, dominance, authenticity, focus, and influence, and it's not just about showing off.

Charisma is a force of human personality that can be understood, measured, and developed. While some people are more naturally charismatic than others, given self-confidence and effort, one can develop charismatic power as a second nature. It's natural for a person to have the capacity to be charismatic because of his or her needs, especially in personal relationships such as dating, mating, and marriage. Charisma helps in many situations in which the person wants to influence other people. It also provides a way to understand and control one's own strength of character.

According to Howard Gardner and Thomas Hatch, (1989), the components of interpersonal intelligence are as follows:

- organizing groups
- negotiating solutions
- personal connection
- social analysis

These are also the ingredients for charm, social success, and charisma. Interpersonal intelligence is the ability to connect with people and understand their thoughts, reactions, and feelings, which makes them easier to lead. A good and popular leader is the one who can leave others with a positive mood and make himself or herself a pleasure to be around.

On the other hand, if a leader applies charisma to fulfill his or her self-interest and narcissistic satisfaction, he or she will be found to be phony and be rejected. Social imposters—those who say one thing and do another—sooner or later will be discovered as leaders without integrity. (For more on unhealthy narcissism, see chapter 5.)

Generally, charisma is a by-product of leadership, stage performance, or public speaking. This could be why, historically, charismatic people have tended to be actors, stage performers, salespeople, religious leaders, politicians, and the like. To an extent, these people become successful in their fields because of charismatic appeal, but charisma here is more often an effect rather than a cause. The main point is that charismatic people tend to come from these backgrounds because these fields require training or experience in effective emotional communications. Charismatic people achieve effectiveness through self-confidence and by engaging, targeting, and inspiring emotional confidence, passion, and empathy. Unfortunately, sometimes the application of charisma is not genuine but motivated by self-interest, especially among some religious leaders and politicians.

Charisma is an acquired capability and an enabling quality, one available to anyone driven by self-motivation and willing to put an effort into technical refinement. Leadership training is also included in personal development, which advances some elements of charisma.

It can be seen that charisma is not supernatural or divinely bestowed or inborn; instead, it is a behavioral quality that anyone can develop. Charisma must embody values, ethics, and feelings. To persuade others, one must use reasoning, moral credibility, and genuine emotions and passions. This is what followers expect from a charismatic leader—to gain a sense of purpose, inspiration, and hope. A charismatic leader needs to learn technical expertise to win the trust of followers and to set strategies to benefit all by achieving goals.

Leadership

A person who is confident, capable and effective, inspiring, and forward thinking; a person who has community knowledge, interpersonal skills, wisdom, values and principles, commitment and determination, good public relations, the ability to establish direction, and skills in strategic planning and execution; a person who is known for his or her courage, honesty, and integrity—such a person is called a leader. A genuine leader who is dedicated to serving humanity becomes a role model and a beacon for all generations. On the other hand, a **sinister leader*** has the opposite characteristics and is the cause of social disharmony, divisiveness, and conflict.

* **Sinister leader** refers to a leader who promotes conflict and fragmentation for his or her own political, religious, and social survival. Such an individual is self-serving, dishonest, domineering, egotistical, divisive, manipulative, and destructive; he or she attracts condemnation. This sort of leader is usually afflicted with personality disorders, especially toxic narcissism, which stems from the feeling of insecurity or inferiority and manifests itself in compulsiveness, manipulation, fibbing, distortion of facts, anxiety, depression, and stress.

Public cynicism and skepticism of political or religious leaders is a healthy approach in countering their application of mass psychology on their constituents, provided that cynicism and skepticism are translated into action. In Western democracies, there is room for vocal and peaceful protests by the silent majority to deter negative leaders from using their superegos and the power of the vocal minority to disadvantage the silent majority. Unfortunately, however, due to political apathy, these powerful democratic tools are not used often enough to enforce people's control of politicians and ultraconservative theologians.

In politics, alarm bells should sound when a political leader becomes more concerned about satisfying vocal minorities and the elite rather than the mainstream majority. It could be to the detriment of the country if people forget that political apathy, especially by the middle class, leads to surrendering the people's power to vested interests and vocal minorities that do not necessarily have the wider national interest as their top priority.

It is detrimental to Western democracy when people's political awareness doesn't extend beyond the biased information presented daily to them by the right-wing media, the press, and manipulative politicians who use mass psychology to meet their objectives. Politicians and religious leaders usually play on people's emotions, ignorance, and insecurity; they exploit people by promoting fear and uncertainty.

It should be understood that by using their emotional and social intelligences, sinister leaders can skillfully mask their real intentions. Their behavior is directed to the establishment of social fears, prejudices, and stereotypes. However, to such leaders, whose only desire is to achieve specific results, emotional intelligence and social intelligence become less relevant and more vulnerable. When this occurs, they can easily be exposed as phony. Unfortunately, they are often able to cause much social damage before they are exposed.

A leader who has a positive attitude and positive behavior and who strives for social harmony tends to attract followers. Followers are naturally drawn to leaders who exhibit strength and can inspire belief. These qualities tend to produce a charismatic effect. Some people are more disposed naturally to leadership than others (see Note below). Most people don't seek to be leaders, but many more people than we realize are able to lead in one way or another and in one situation or another. People who want to be leaders can develop leadership ability by developing emotional intelligence, especially in the area of emotional control, which results in staying focused and clearheaded under pressure. Leadership is the ability to take people where they don't always want to go, and, at the same time, it is the ability to bring people together. Leadership is about having vision and the ability to communicate with others about the process for achieving that vision. Ultimately, leadership is about uniting people who have different ideas and who come from different directions.

> **Note:** Genetic scientists have uncovered evidence that born leaders actually exist—rs4950, an inherited DNA sequence associated in some people with the capacity to manage or lead. The lead scientist,

Jan-Emmanuel De Neve from University College London, in January 2013, said, "We have identified a genotype, called rs4950, which appears to be associated with the passing of leadership ability down through generations." A study on four thousand individuals, which matched them to their actual jobs, found that a quarter of the observed variation in leadership traits between individuals could be explained by genetics.

Scientists accept that leadership skills are learned; however, the presence of the gene helps to make someone a leader or manager. That leadership is a skill still remains largely true, but in part, it is genetic. Ultimately, despite the importance of the gene, leadership still mostly depends on developing the necessary skills, say the researchers. However, more research is needed to understand the ways the gene interacts with other factors, such as one's learning environment and method of education.

To achieve positive results, a leader should be knowledgeable, perceptive, honest, efficient, fast thinking, and able to communicate effectively. Given these criteria, many people are capable of being leaders, provided they are provided with **leadership development**** and equal opportunity to acquire knowledge, communication skills, and reasoning through comprehensive and affordable education at all levels.

** *Leadership development:* Effective leadership does not neces-sarily require great technical or intellectual capacity. These attributes might help, but they are not pivotal. Understanding the nature of good leadership is much easier than practicing it because good leadership needs qualities that go beyond the ability to exercise authority. A leader must have the ability to enable others to perform, develop, and achieve. Without becoming a role model in attitude, behavior, and dedication to the cause of serving the people, a leader becomes ineffective or character-ized as sinister—one who seeks out opportunities for personal gain at the expense of others.

Instead of being opportunistic, a true leader is mentally geared up to serve his or her organization and generally the people. Based on ancient philosophy and in accor-dance with a 1970 essay by Robert Greenleaf, the idea of "servant leader and servant leadership" is the concept of a leader being one who serves a function rather than one who is served. A leader with mental and emotional strength is mostly concerned with others, and his or her skills and knowledge are devoted to helping others. A true leader is committed and responsible. An effec-tive leader is followed and revered because he or she is trusted and respected, more so for that person's behav-ior and integrity than for his or her skills and knowledge. A leader mostly relies on intangible aspects of interper-sonal relationships, such as trust, conviction, wisdom, and the ability to make decisions, develop processes, and inspire others.

A good leader is equipped with a disciplined personal response to a range of situations and experiences. In other words, he or she is in total control of his or her impulses, which is an essential element in successful human relations. Understanding rational and irrational human behavior in a complex society is an artistic sensibility that depends on the person's inherited or learned brilliance. It is a leadership quality, the ability to analyze and apply skills when dealing with others, which stems from thinking and learning.

As can be seen, many people are suited to become leaders, and occasionally a positive and exceptional one emerges who can lead a nation in a complex and frag- mented world. All such a leader needs is some intel- ligence—including emotional intelligence and social intelligence—knowledge, and experience. In the last two decades, a significant amount of research has been done to identify relationships between emotional intelligence and social intelligence regarding life satisfaction, personal- ity, and social relationships. Modern leaders are confronted by many imperatives of the changing realities driven by social, political, economic, and technological changes. The world is in desperate need of new leaders to meet these new realities. For example, the current state of interna- tional relations is in desperate need of moderate leaders to avert the total fragmentation of the world. (For more on international relations, see my book, *Israel vs. America vs. the World.*)

On the local front, leaders should be equipped to deal with modern daily environments, events, and behaviors, such as shifting moral values, the impact of consumerism, the impact of politics, changing social attitudes, and, most important, the impact of social media and cybertechnologies. All of these create different challenges, which in turn require new leaders with new states of mind and social intelligence and different leadership characteristics, especially in their self-awareness, capacity to influence others, and level of motivation and integrity. An emotionally intelligent leader knows how to manage his or her emotions, stays focused, thinks clearly, stays flexible and optimistic, and has superior communication ability.

The Impact of Extreme Capitalism

Social intelligence is affected by the extreme greed associated with extreme capitalism. This greed, which lacks all regard for proper human relations, results in one person becoming richer at the expense of many others. When the rich get richer and the poor get poorer, resentment develops to an extent that often ends in social revolt and upheaval. Long-term extreme capitalism can destroy the social fabric and eventually lead to its own brutal elimination. It's like the law of physics that states that one extreme creates the opposite extreme. This is what caused the Russian Revolution, which was a revolt of the exploited against the exploiters. The revolution unfortunately created an economic system of the socialist extreme whereby the incentive to achieve and the spirit of competition were destroyed and eventually everybody got poorer. In the absence of wise leadership that is equipped with social intelligence, the socialist system collapsed and will be followed by extreme capitalism. Perhaps a moderate economic system between the two extremes is the answer. The moderate system should be based on fair distribution of wealth without removing the spirit of competition and the incentive to achieve. The system is called "Social Democracy."

The current state of affairs in the United States is an example of extreme capitalism: leaders are blinded by short-term self-interest rather than worrying about the eventual consequences that have the potential to destroy their own country and their own wealth.

Describing extreme capitalism in *Israel vs. America vs. the World*, (2011), I wrote the following:

> Extreme capitalism in which the rich get richer and the poor get poorer is in contrast with socialism where everybody gets poorer. It is fundamentally based on the creation of economic power through political power and implemented by the middle class to exploit the masses and other nations. It has a built-in self-destruct mechanism called *excess credit*. Some aspects of excess credit can be observed in nations and corporations

borrowing well in excess of what they earn, which ultimately results in defaults. Often excess credit extends to the average citizen, with similar outcome. Excessive borrowing often results in financial crisis because the survival of the capitalist system depends on spending, and when the spending stops, so does the system.

Big spending that is fuelled by financial engineering for the benefit of a few, as in the recent financial disaster, will force many countries, especially the United States and Europe, to stabilize their debt. To fund their liability, they resort to printing money to revive their economies, which sets the ground for a new round of inflation and possibly hyperinflation. Alternatively, some countries default or raise taxes to pay debt. Raising taxes leads to economic stagnation, higher unemployment, slower growth, and generally weaker economic outcomes.

In its quest for profit without taking into account morals and human values, extreme capitalism creates many losers and resentful underclass social groups, which results in social instability and eventual revolt, whether large- or small-scale. But social stability can be achieved: one way is by the fair distribution of wealth, which begins with providing equal opportunity to all children to reach their full potential through free and quality education.

One of the most damaging aspects of extreme capitalism is that the owners of capital and vested interests control the system to the extent that politicians cannot innovate and reform without their approval. Worse yet is an interdependency of religion and politics, for this results in the suffocation of social progress and the triumph of conformism over individualism. Conformism is the main factor behind the retardation of creativity and innovation. (For more on conformism and individualism, see chapter 5 of my book *Death by Choice versus Religious Dogma*.)

In the United States, extreme capitalism has turned the financial markets into a gravy train for the executives and their boards of directors while investors and workers are relegated to the bottom of the food chain. This greed will eventually lead to the destruction of the very system that engendered it, a system that is producing megafinancial institutions. Goldman Sachs—considered the smartest, greediest, and most dangerous investment bank, together with a few other major US financial institutions—is at the head of the cartel that is causing a calamity. Their admission of guilt requires the pursuit of justice, and their actions should be considered domestic and international terrorism—not with deadly guns, but with deadly money—and treated accordingly. In their pursuit of money, these institutions have destroyed the nation's wealth and created many victims, all to line their own pockets. The United States is saddled with huge financial institutions that are too big to fail, with managers that are too powerful to sue. These managers believe in the fiction that under capitalism the market regulates itself and that if they inflate asset prices, those prices will eventually go back to fair value. In the process, they line their pockets while the poor get poorer. The free market was never meant to be a free license to take whatever you can get however you can get it. Extreme capitalists, lacking social intelligence and blinded by their short-term advantage, forget that the poorer the majority becomes, the nearer the revolt gets. It must be frightening for Americans to live in a country where over three hundred million guns—including assault rifles—are in the hands of an unhappy people who may one day revolt. (For more on gun violence, see chapter 7.)

What happened in the United States was the result of turning a blind eye on the financial institutions' speculative investment, lack of risk assessment, rampant credit growth, and inflated asset prices. An economic system in which financial institutions indulge in rigging the market without fear and for maximum gains for their elite managers is doomed. These institutions, together with other major enterprises, got engaged in schemes to minimize and avoid taxes by using loopholes and offshore tax havens. Within this growing financial system, large banks and corporations that expected to be bailed out by the government were encouraged to take bigger risks—which resulted in greater damage. The by-products of this system were extreme greed and the unfair distribution of wealth. These were magnified by the recession, which showed the widening gap between the rich and the poor. It also showed the United States to have the greatest disparity between the rich and the poor of all industrialized nations.

Under extreme capitalism, even the rating agencies become concerned with their own profit rather than following their charter of total honesty and professionalism. In the wake of the 2008 financial crisis, the Department of Justice stated that Wall Street's largest credit rating agency, Standard & Poor's, was accused of knowingly committing fraud by issuing falsely inflated credit ratings between 2004 and 2007.

From internal S&P e-mails, it became apparent that the agency was knowingly not giving objective credit ratings for the sake of retaining clients and increasing profits. They knew they were rating junk but saying it was high quality, and this caused big losses for many companies and individuals who relied on and trusted those ratings. S&P promised investors and the public that their ratings were based on data and analytical models reflecting the company's true credit judgment when, in fact, internal S&P documents make clear that the company would regularly tweak, bend, delay updating, or otherwise adjust its ratings models to suit the company's business needs. They repeatedly misrepresented their ratings, claiming they were independent and objective when, in fact, they were largely skewed, motivated by a desire to retain clients, gain market share, and increase profits.

It appeared that the rating agencies were not independent, and they were not objective. Many pension funds and mutual funds purchase investment vehicles only if they are highly rated. These funds and other investors were misled into mortgage-backed investment and subprime loans that were given the highest AAA rating, and this was one of the main causes of the economic collapse. Three rating agencies, S&P, Moody's, and Fitch, are being sued in the United States and in other countries for the damage they caused, especially in granting triple-A and double-A ratings to collateralized debt obligations (CDOs) sold by investment banks. (CDOs are a type of structured bank security characterized by multiple "tranches" of debt largely built up from US home loans. It was one of the causes of the global financial crisis). Potential legal cases in Europe and elsewhere could leave these agencies broke, especially considering that the claims could exceed their net tangible assets. Accordingly, they most likely will not get the support of the capital markets, as they will be considered a credit risk.

Extreme greed generated by extreme capitalism brought with it the erosion of ethics, social destruction, and the corruption of human relations. Capitalism is good if people and governments don't spend more than they have or at least adhere to an affordable borrowing policy. Too much borrowing, especially against inflated asset prices, is a recipe for financial crisis. It appears that the simple lesson that excessive greed is destructive is one that human beings are incapable of learning. Ultragreed is fuelling a silent revolution as Americans continue to lose their jobs and homes, and millions of people are unable to find work or are becoming underemployed and are struggling to survive at minimum-wage jobs.

Worse still, because of the great divergence, the stagnation of middle-class income will have a major impact on the United States' future growth. History shows that the destruction of the middle class in any country has a long-term destructive effect on its economy. All this destruction is carried out to satisfy the greed of a select few who promote extreme capitalism and sponsor extreme or opportunistic politicians to prevent the fair distribution of wealth. They prevent or corrupt any regulation that may interfere with their selfish endeavor.

A study by Harvard University based on 2009 economic data shows the following reality:

> The gap between the United States' rich and poor has widened dramatically. The wealth of $54 trillion dollars, in 2009, was divided among 311 Americans, which highlights the problem of the inequitable distribution of wealth. It also shows that the bottom 40 percent of Americans barely has any of the wealth at all, and the middle class is barely distinguishable from the poor. The top 2 to 5 percent of Americans are so rich they go off the chart, and the top 1 percent is so rich they get a chart of their own. The shocking part is that 80 percent of Americans only have 7 percent of the wealth between them. This is compared to 1976 when the richest 1 percent only took home 9 percent of the wealth—now they take home 24 percent. Furthermore,

the average CEO is earning 380 times more
than the average employee (not the lowest-
paid employee—the average one).

The United States is in desperate need of a new economic
model and policies that focus on recovering the middle
class and raising the minimum wage to recover the nation's
spending power. But due to partisan politics and lack
of understanding, the Republican Party has made itself
a stumbling block, preventing any reform that doesn't
make the rich richer and the poor poorer. For example, the
Republicans often advance the argument that raising the
minimum wage causes businesses to cut jobs because they
can no longer afford to pay all of their workers. Here the
Republicans' argument doesn't take into consideration that
when the economy is in recession, it has to be stimulated
by additional spending. To stimulate spending depends
largely on improving people's spending power to increase
demand, while the opposite is happening when the working and the middle class are getting poorer and when their
wages are depressed. Furthermore, spending cannot be
stimulated when the United States has the greatest concentration of wealth in the top 2 percent of the population.
And this is when the unfair redistribution of wealth is making the United States a country where upward mobility is
no longer in sight and where investment in the future is
drastically diminished.

The United States is a country where extreme capitalism
has caused great inequality and now poses a great threat

to democracy. In addition, the Republican Party is successfully destroying the concept that the United States was built on: if you work hard and meet your responsibilities, you will be rewarded. It is unfortunate for the United States to have a political party that believes that capitalism means everybody must fend for himself, a philosophy that is based on the principle of sink or swim. This concept of capitalism means that the disadvantaged and the unemployed are left behind to fend for themselves without a safety net. It doesn't take into consideration the consequences of adopting new technologies, which causes some workers and managers to become redundant. Some are afforded the opportunity of retraining, and others miss out. Some are capable of adapting, and some are not. Without providing a safety net and adequate social security, the capitalist system leaves many people behind with nothing left to do but beg, turn to crime, or ultimately revolt. Extreme capitalism has already left forty-five million Americans living below the poverty line, and still more are becoming trapped in entrenched poverty. Worse yet, many Americans working full-time are living below the poverty line because of depressed wages. Despite this, the Republicans oppose any increase to the minimum hourly rate. Despite being members of a party of theocracy, for all their biblical inspirations, the Republicans don't seem to understand the meaning of social justice.

The entrenchment of poverty is the first ingredient of social disintegration and the seed of eventual upheaval and revolt. It's the unfortunate outcome of sinister leadership that is devoid of social intelligence.

The Republican Party doesn't understand that when the rich get richer and the poor get poorer, a social disparity develops that culminates in major discontent and becomes the cause of upheaval. The history of revolutions suggests that what happened in other countries will happen in the United States, no matter how farfetched this thought might sound now. With the existence of three hundred million assault rifles in the United States, upheaval can create killing fields in the battle for survival and the survival of the fittest or the desperate. The history of revolutions also shows that when a major social vacuum is created and an underclass is established that has nothing left to lose, an upheaval follows. (The law of physics, too, says that a vacuum will be filled.)

The Republican Party also doesn't understand that when the middle class and the poor are poorer, the purchasing power of the nation gets eroded. Consumer spending growth usually is driven mostly by the growth in households' income, consumers' confidence, and their wealth. A capitalist system in a developed economy depends largely on spending, and when spending stops, the economy goes into recession. Furthermore, if wages are continuously depressed—for the rich to get richer—the incentive to improve productivity on the management side proportionally diminishes. The drive to meet international competition dictates that management adopts innovations, invests in new technologies, improves systems, and generally cuts costs. Depressing wages results in removing the incentive from manufacturers to aim for restructuring as a method of boosting efficiency and productivity. Destroying the incentive of the workforce by cutting wages is counterproductive. Extreme capitalism that is advocated by the Republicans creates extremely rich managers. Some of those managers and executives are motivated by reward and status, and others by avoiding punishment. This is especially so in the financial sector, most prominently in investment banking, which was exposed during the financial crisis. (For more on The Tea Party Movement and the Republicans, see below.)

Moderate capitalism, on the other hand, is based on moderate greed, where give-and-take and win-win principles apply and where the creation and fair distribution of wealth is an essential element. It is in contrast with extreme capitalism, which lines the pockets of a select few and leaves the weak and the vulnerable to fend for themselves. Under moderate capitalism, governments don't spend more than what they have or they at least adhere to an affordable borrowing policy. Moderate governments retain the flexibility and the capacity to step in during economic slowdowns and periods of high unemployment to protect the country and its most vulnerable people from social upheaval.

Capitalism as an economic system is a good thing, but when it crosses over to the dark side, it no longer is. In fact it becomes extremely dangerous, especially when it controls the political system of the nation, becomes expansionist, and applies aggression in its endeavor to control other nations. This can be illustrated by the United States' current brutal approach to international relations, which is causing many casualties and the devastation of other nations' infrastructures. In the name of fighting terrorism (while hiding their ambition of economic expansion and control of the world's energy resources), the United States is engaged—directly or indirectly—in the slaughter of many innocent people. The United States doesn't understand that influence, not power, is ultimately the most valuable strategy. Influence comes from magnanimity and reaps greater gains. The use of power results in resentment and reaction, which ultimately weakens and destroys the aggressor. Just look at the history of the rise and fall of empires. (For more on the rise and fall of empires, see chapter 1 of *Israel vs. America vs. the World*.)

Despite the setbacks, the United States still doesn't understand that its decline is caused by the process of waging wars and borrowing money to fight those wars, which will ultimately lead to its demise. The United States currently has an unsustainable public debt, largely incurred to finance unnecessary wars, the reduction of which is hindered by a nasty partisan political structure and politicians who lack social intelligence and wisdom. In the meantime, the country is printing money until hyperinflation catches up with it. Worse yet, while funding is directed to wars, other essential growth factors are ignored, such as education, science, health, and infrastructures—these are the essential elements of progress and prosperity.

Having adopted extreme capitalism, the United States now needs continuous market expansion in addition to a continuous supply of cheap energy sources. Furthermore, its economic reliance on arms manufacturing is forcing the country to engineer continuous conflicts around the world to create demand and markets for its military hardware and associated technologies.

The hidden agenda of extreme capitalism is to control other countries and their people. In the process of adopting extreme capitalism and expansionist policies and since winning the Cold War and becoming the world's only superpower, the United States has turned to aggressive military and foreign policies. This brings it into conflict with nations that resist economic exploitation, and this is amplified by the presence of religious and cultural clashes. From the history of the rise and fall of empires, we can see that the presence of these elements leads to violent confrontation. Again, the principle of one extreme creating the other—which coincides with the law of physics that states that every action provokes an equal reaction—is at work.

Without admitting its aggression, the United States pretends to be an innocent bystander and an unfair target of Islamic terrorism. Now the empire calls the enemies of its own creation "terrorists." Despite its pretention, however, the world is well aware of how this purportedly innocent empire managed to kill half a million Iraqis to rid the world of nonexistent weapons of mass destruction. This is the way the empire hides its real reasons and its need to control the energy supplies and other countries' resources. (For more on the Iraq War, see my book *Israel vs. America vs. the World*.) Unfortunately, this is the way of the US empire: create enemies and call them terrorists that must be exterminated. Propaganda plays a key role in creating who the good and the bad are—who should live and who should die. And the right-wing media and press are the major tools at the extreme capitalists' disposal. (By the way, the extreme capitalists own and manage the majority of these propaganda tools.)

Worse still, to fight these terrorists, the empire employs every possible technology at its disposal, including phone tapping and fund transfers, and it extends these practices to its own citizens and to all citizens of the world. In spying on the country's citizens, the United States is eroding its citizens' civil liberties and destroying the country's democracy. According to American Civil Liberties Union (ACLU), wiretapping Americans is in clear violation of the law.

However, it is understandable that under extreme capitalism, the concept of democracy doesn't exist; it didn't exist under socialism, either. The government that is representing the interest of 2 percent of the population wants to know everything possible about every citizen in the event of future class struggles or major upheavals that may eventuate as a consequence of the rich getting richer and the poor getting poorer. Using the excuse that it is finding the balance between keeping Americans safe and fighting terrorism, it achieves this objective by having access to gigantic databases and spying on everything and everyone in the world, including its allies and its own citizens. The communication records of millions of American and European citizens are being collected indiscriminately and in bulk—regardless of whether those individuals are suspected of any wrongdoing. No matter how friendly and innocent they may appear, institutions and websites such as banks, phone companies, Microsoft, Google, Yahoo, Facebook, YouTube, Skype, Apple, Twitter, and various Internet and e-mail providers have extremely vulnerable information. The National Security Agency, under the pretense of keeping the United States safe, can access any information from them whenever it desires, and these organizations have no option but to oblige. The questions to be asked are these: What business does the government have in the private affairs of its citizens? What right does any government have to invade individuals' privacy? Furthermore, the Internet and all these institutions are international networks—used by people all over the world—which results in the NSA's indiscriminate violation of privacy of every citizen in the world.

Worse yet, according to a top-secret agreement disclosed by US intelligence whistleblower Edward Snowden that NSA routinely shares intelligence data with Israel without first sifting through it to remove information about US citizens and the citizens of US's close allies. Details of intelligence-sharing between the NSA and its Israeli counterpart, the Israeli Signals Intelligence National Unit, published by *The Guardian* newspaper show the US government hands over to Israel "raw" or "unevaluated and unminimised" signals intelligence including "transcripts, gist, facsimiles, telex, voice and Digital Network Intelligence (DNI) metadata and content." With much of the world's internet traffic passing through America's telecommunications networks, large volumes of purely US domestic communications as well as the communications of US allies are collected by the NSA's surveillance programs. If this doesn't alarm Western countries' citizens about the loss of their privacy and civil liberties; what will?

All the spying is coupled with the administration's huge appetite for secrecy of information and intelligence. This is characteristic of the epidemic culture of governing under extreme capitalism, which is identical to the culture of extreme socialism as was demonstrated under the Soviet Union's KGB and East Germany's Stasi. In both cases, all information was classified because of national security. Socialist and extreme capitalist systems with their security apparatus go out of their way to spy on their citizens and to keep their nation in the dark.

All citizens must understand that the data collected and stored by a government they may trust today can be used against them by a nasty government they don't trust tomorrow. Above all, the government people are trusting today is deceiving the nation, and its survival depends on telling lies. This is confirmed by the recent revelation that the FBI is using drones and phone tapping to spy on Americans. The government states that the secret use of drones is very limited. If people are naïve enough to trust this government that bends the Constitution to suit itself, what will stop a nastier government in the future from bending it further to the detriment of future generations' civil liberties? With the power of money, election of a nastier government is not out of the question. Furthermore, the trusted government of today is elected and owned by extreme capitalists.

On the subject of one extreme creating the opposite extreme, in *Israel vs. America vs. the World*, (2011), I wrote the following:

> The United States has a choice, to continue with its costly wars and self-destruction or to create a peaceful world that is built on a win-win principle instead of its current winner-takes-all principle. Prosperity instead of its current decline can be achieved by adopting a moderate capitalism that embodies the fair distribution of wealth and by rejecting extreme capitalism that leads to the rich getting richer and the poor getting poorer. The culture and psychology of moderate capitalism will lead to give-and-take as a better guiding principle to human and international relations. The starting point for the United States to become a reasonable country is by its developing exit strategies to end the unnecessary wars against Islamic countries. First, it needs to remove the majority of its military bases from around the world that are set up to attack other nations rather than defend the United States, especially the ones that provoke resentment and insurgency. Second, it must act decisively to establish a viable Palestinian state. Third, it needs to clean up the CIA, which is acting inhumanely and is out of control and acting as a government within a

government. The United States has a choice: to stay the course as an expansionist empire but in decline or to become a great empire. To be a great empire is to allow poorer countries to prosper and for more people to become consumers instead of refugees or enemies of the empire.

For a capitalist system to succeed, a moderate greed under moderate capitalism should be taught at an early age through intelligent conditioning. It is idealistic to fight greed and to brand it as guilt since it is part of human nature and the human survival instinct. It is natural for humans to be motivated by beauty, dignity, a desire for security, and happiness. It is also natural for humans to want more than a fair share. There should be a legitimate way, however, to possess things, provided it's based on a win-win principle. This can be achieved by self-understanding and the understanding of others based on knowledge and behavioral science, which should be part of school curricula.

Extreme capitalism as currently practiced in the United States, where competition is cutthroat and contributes to the social conflict, is one of the causes of the high number of school dropouts. Such conditions, coupled with the availability of firearms, constitute some of the ingredients for high levels of crime and violence.

In The Price of Civilisation: Reawakening American Virtue and Prosperity, (2012), by Jeffrey D. Sachs, an economist from Columbia University, he wrote, "The US economy is caught in a feedback loop. Corporate wealth translates into political power through campaign financing, corporate lobbying, and the revolving door of jobs between government and industry; and political power translates into further wealth through tax cuts, deregulation, and sweetheart contracts between government and industry. Wealth begets power, and power begets wealth." He added, "Four key sectors of US business exemplify this feedback loop and the takeover of political power in the United States by the corporatocracy—a political system in which powerful corporate interest groups dominate the policy agenda." He explained the four key sectors as follows:

- First is the military-industrial complex, which President Eisenhower famously warned about in his farewell address in January 1961. The linkage of the military and private industry created a political power so pervasive that the United States has been condemned to militarization, useless wars, and fiscal waste on a scale of many tens of trillions of dollars since then.

- Second is the Wall Street-Washington complex, which has steered the financial system toward control by a few politically powerful Wall Street firms, notably Goldman Sachs, JPMorgan Chase, Citigroup, Morgan Stanley, and a handful of others. These days, almost every US Treasury secretary—Republican or Democrat—comes from Wall Street and goes back there when his or her term ends. According to Sachs, the close ties between Wall Street and Washington "paved the way for the 2008 financial crisis and the mega-bailouts that followed, through reckless deregulation followed by an almost complete lack of oversight by government."

• Third, the Big Oil-transport-military complex has put the United States on the trajectory of heavy oil-imports dependence and a deepening military trap in the Middle East. Since the days of John D. Rockefeller and the Standard Oil Trust a century ago, Big Oil has loomed large in US politics and foreign policy. Big Oil teamed up with the automobile industry to steer the United States away from mass transit and toward gas-guzzling vehicles driving on a nationally financed highway system.

Big Oil has consistently and successfully fought the intrusion of competition from (non-oil) energy sources, including nuclear, wind, and solar power. It has been at the side of the Pentagon in making sure that the United States defends the sea-lanes to the Persian Gulf, in effect ensuring a $100 billion-plus annual subsidy for a fuel that is otherwise dangerous for national security. Sachs says, "And Big Oil has played a notorious role in the fight to keep climate change off the US agenda. Exxon-Mobil, Koch Industries, and others in the sector have underwritten a generation of anti-scientific propaganda to confuse the American people."

- Fourth, the health care industry, the United States' largest industry, is absorbing no less than 17 percent of US gross domestic product. "The key to understanding this sector is to note that the government partners with industry to reimburse costs with little systematic oversight and control." Pharmaceutical firms set sky-high prices protected by patent rights—Medicare for the aged and Medicaid for the poor—and private insurers reimburse doctors and hospitals on a cost-plus basis, and the American Medical Association restricts the supply of new doctors through the control of placements at medical schools.

The results of this pseudomarket system are sky-high costs, large profits for the private health care sector, and no political will to reform. Jeffrey Sachs says the main thing to remember about the corporatocracy is that it looks after its own. There is absolutely no economic crisis in corporate United States. Consider the pulse of the corporate sector as opposed to the pulse of the employees working in it. Corporate profits in 2010 were at an all-time high, and chief executive salaries in 2010 rebounded strongly from the financial crisis. Wall Street compensation in 2010 was at an all-time high, and although several Wall Street firms paid civil penalties for financial abuses, no senior banker faced any criminal charges, and there were no adverse regulatory measures that would lead to a loss of profits in finance, health care, military supplies, and energy. The thirty-year achievement of the corporatocracy has been the creation of the United States' rich and super-rich classes.

The Tea Party and the Republicans

The Tea Party is another reason behind the absence of emotional and social intelligences in the United States' leadership. It's a loosely organized movement of extreme right-wing political groups and individuals. An extremely conservative wing of the Republican Party, its ideology, which is based on theology, advocates a form of capitalism that favors the rich. It motivates its followers with slogans such as, "Constitutionally limited government supports maximum individual liberty." The behavior of its adherents, however, indicates that the liberty they are after is for the Rights and the extreme Rights, but not for anyone else. Its religious commitment is making the Republican Party a party of theocracy, whereby religion and politics become inseparable.

The Tea Party is the driving force behind the political polarization in the United States, and the polarization between the Republican and Democrat parties is gradually leading the United States to self-destruction. Earlier, Congress operated more on a conscience-vote basis, but because of the control exerted on the Republican Party by the extremist Tea Party, the voting system is now strictly based on party loyalty. It's now seldom that members of

Congress vote as independent or to represent their constituencies in an appropriate way. Republicans' toeing the party line is driving the Democrats to do the same, hence the polarization. There is no logic, for example, when one party has the capacity to veto tax increases while the other party has the capacity to veto spending cuts. One of them must be wrong, and the truth may lie between the two. The previous capacity of Congress to hear the voices of minorities is now lost. The move to party authoritarianism usually results in placing the political power in the hands of a few influential members of the party, which makes a mockery out of any democracy.

Partisan politics is the politics of conflict rather than conflict resolution, which is the practice the education system is meant to teach through emotional intelligence. Unfortunately, in this instance, politicians become the worst role models for the younger generation that, in turn, learns and develops the feeling of brinkmanship. Political brinkmanship is a form of political violence that reflects the nation's psyche and could contribute to polarization and violence between individuals as it sets the example and the mood for conflict. Furthermore, this brinkmanship is extended to the international stage, which is another cause for concern because it doesn't allow for peaceful conflict resolution in the world, and this drives the nation toward violence against other nations.

Brinkmanship and a dysfunctional system of government have a negative effect on the nation's psyche. Partisan politics place the interest of one political party and its ideology above the interest of the country, especially when one party is determined to defeat the other at all costs. The political polarization and the constant use of the filibuster rule in the Senate to obstruct legislation (even when it is in the United States' national interest) impedes the country's progress and makes it unable to solve pressing problems. The desperately needed spirits of compromise and moderation have disappeared, which is the main cause for America's decline.

The constitutional rules of filibuster were originally designed so that debating legislations could reach a better outcome for the country; they now have the opposite effect. Unfortunately, the ideology-driven interest of one party is becoming more important than the country. The Republican Party, driven by the extremist Tea Party under the political slogan "We're taking back the country from the Socialists," is having a major impact on political, social, and economic outcomes in the United States. Partisanship and brinkmanship have turned the United States into a country in a state of psychological depression and economic stagnation from which a bipartisan approach is the only way out. But unfortunately, its corrupted democracy—driven by money and religion—is hindering it from moving forward, and politicians lack leadership and social intelligence. As it stands, to restore America's prosperity is by getting rid of the extreme Right ideologies, which entails the rejection of the Tea Party that is driving America to the brink, or to the edge of the cliff. (For more on the Tea Party, see my book *Israel vs. America vs. the World.*)

CHAPTER 4

Wisdom

Definition

Wisdom is considered a virtue of intellect, and it is the force behind ethical, harmonious, and rational human relations. Enlightened people define wisdom as a combination of knowledge, reasoning, experience, and **common sense.** * Wisdom was, still is, and should always be humanity's guide. It allows us to survive amid conflicts and wars spurred by the desire for domination over and exploitation of other nations that some extremists, megalomaniacs, and overambitious world leaders have.

* **Common sense** is used here as a conscious understanding of the world that improves people's perception, behavior, planning, and communication.

Wisdom leads to harmonious human relations because it embodies ethical principles based on the virtues of reciprocal, material, and intellectual exchange. The gradual softening of human aggression and its replacement with intellectual exchange enhances civilization; in fact, this is the key to human social evolution and the guarantee of survival. Wisdom gives us the capacity to realize what is of value in life. It helps us to use new knowledge and technological advances to increase human power, attain positive goals, and prevent unnecessary suffering and death.

A wise person has his or her knowledge and experience well coordinated, making him or her sincere, direct, consultative, and ethical. A wise person is also equipped with the power of comprehension and the ability to analyze what is true and what is false, as well as to make the best judgment before action. To be wise is to consider causes rather than to act rashly or indulgently. According to the Inuit Elders-Wisdom Quotes website, "The person becomes wise when he or she can see what is needed to be done and do it successfully without being told what to do." And according to the Native American Philosophy website, "Wisdom is about maintaining balance ecologically and socially and a common sense approach to protecting and conserving natural resources."

On the other hand, according to the old religious definition, "Wisdom is related to people seeking immortality through God, whilst the lack of wisdom is related to the ungodly, who faced a miserable fate." This definition contradicts the modern definition of wisdom as knowledge, reasoning, experience, and the conscious understanding of the world.

Wisdom and Culture

Wisdom being the human virtue of intellect, it embodies the interdependence of knowledge, reasoning, and experience, and this interdependence will always be the ultimate guide to human survival. Wisdom guides us to the common sense principle of flexible moderation, which allows for diversity in social environments and in each individual's intellectual creativity. Applying flexible moderation means taking into consideration the emphasis, definition, and interpretation of meanings assigned to values in many cultures, and this could be the best path to harmonious human relations.

Wisdom, an essential part of culture, can be defined as an evolutionary social process that coincides with the sophistication of people relative to their scientific and economic progress. It encompasses all aspects of life, especially customs, traditions, religion, arts, language, common sense, and scientific and technological achievements. Common sense and scientific and technological achievements are the mental components of culture, while customs, traditions, arts, and religion are the spiritual components. Wisdom, generally, is the catalyst between all components.

Variation and degree of emphasis in the above components within various groups and nations are the determining factors behind the world's multicultural structure. A single common and homogeneous culture in one society leads to social stability, while in a multicultural society, social friction might arise as a result of insecurity. This friction is mainly fuelled by political and religious leaders, who have a vested interest in engineering social behavior to maintain their prominence and dominance.

Here it is important to emphasize again that through secular education and experience, people can develop intuition, perception, common sense, spontaneity, free expression, creativity, and a free spirit devoid of religion, negative politics, prejudice, and irrationality. Good citizenship occurs when people accept one another and reject discrimination. A good politician is one who constantly promotes equality, individuality, diversity, and fair-go principles.

Fair-go, however, has a different meaning to different people: what it means to the unscrupulous employers who exploit their employees is not what it means to those exploited employees. The fair-go principle doesn't apply under extreme capitalism, in which the rich get richer and the poor get poorer. What is a fair-go to the people who have been left behind by society and discriminated against by the privileged rich for many decades?

The Western world is mature enough to develop a secular school curriculum for teaching logic, rational thinking, common sense, and associated subjects to develop a new generation of nation builders equipped with wisdom, common sense, and objectivity.

Knowledge and Experience

Knowledge

Knowledge is all that is learned directly or indirectly by conclusions and deductions based on science, rules of logic, common sense, and common facts. It's a process of understanding tangibles, intangibles, perception, and reasoning and arriving at logical conclusions based on one's experience, the experience of others, and historical events. Knowledge also relates to the education of people in the application of facts, information, descriptions, practical understanding, and all acquired skills for the development of a nation.

Plato (428–348 BC) defined knowledge as "justified true belief"; Bertrand Russell (1872–1970) called it a theory. Since belief is difficult to define and a theory is more philosophical than scientific, it becomes difficult to accept these definitions. The debate over the definition is ongoing, but in the age of modern science, knowledge could be relatively defined by its tangible and intangible aspects, which mainly relate to economic prosperity and social prosperity, respectively. Social prosperity relates to behavior, values, and human relations that are constantly modified and transmitted from one generation to another. The social and environmental conditions of a group are behind the emergence and development of culture, which determines the system of interaction between and among people.

The bridge between all definitions, the old and the new, is language, the medium of communication between people. Language, both oral and written, is subject to evolution relative to social and scientific progress. Written language is the key to the transfer of technical information and for improving the memory of the following generations. Oral language, in some cases, lends itself to the spread of falsehoods and provokes skepticism. Writing is still the most universal and the most useful of all forms of recording and transmitting knowledge. It stands unchallenged as the primary technology of knowledge transfer down through the ages and to all cultures of the world.

Some methods of generating knowledge are based on trial and error, which means that learning is acquired through experience. Such learning is termed as "afterward knowledge." Other methods of generating knowledge are based on theories and are termed as "prior knowledge." Prior knowledge of an experience allows one to make certain assumptions by taking things for granted.

Scientific methods have made a significant contribution to the way knowledge is acquired. To be termed scientific, a method of inquiry must be based on gathering observable and measurable evidence subject to specific principles of reasoning and experimentation. The scientific method consists of the collection of data through observation and experimentation and the formulation and testing of hypotheses. Science is the process used to logically complete thoughts through inference of facts determined by calculated experiments.

Scientific knowledge may not involve a claim to certainty; maintaining skepticism means that scientists will never be absolutely certain whether they are correct or not. This is because science is based on doubt, and its progress depends on the idea that when different facts are presented, the conclusions change accordingly. Scientific knowledge is based on doubt even when correct, in the hope for better findings. This reflects humankind's inquiring mind, which constantly searches for answers and will not be satisfied with today's conclusion; it always strives for a better one tomorrow. Humans are motivated by curiosity to discover and to apply their discoveries to improve their lives and their chances of survival.

As stated earlier, scientific knowledge is the opposite of religious knowledge, which is based on absolutism and fairy tales. Christianity names knowledge "one of the seven gifts of the Holy Spirit." And the Old Testament (Genesis 3:22) suggests a similar origin: the "tree of the knowledge of good and evil contained the knowledge that separated Man from God: And the Lord God said, behold, the man is become as one of us, to know good and evil..." These and many biblical stories make it easy to see that accepting religious ideologies and mythologies blindly, without questioning, can mean shutting down the brain's usual and critical thinking processes.

Experience

Experience is all that has been developed and accumulated, consciously and unconsciously, directly from our own learning, or indirectly from others through shared learning.

- Benjamin Franklin said, "Experience is the best teacher, but a fool will learn from no other."

- Julius Caesar said, "Experience is the teacher of all things."

The best teacher may be conscious observation, which includes observing one's responses to one's own and others' experiences. Conscious observation is also the awareness of past and present, and it is part of self-image and personality. However, the best teacher could also be the one who can listen and step beyond his or her own personality, which in many instances is narrow or limited. The ability to go beyond one's personality demonstrates wide experience and wisdom, which is gained as a result of a slow evolutionary process that includes many tragedies and triumphs. (For more on self-image, see chapter 5.)

Experience as a general concept comprises knowledge of or skill in something or some event gained through involvement in or exposure to that thing or event. Schools by themselves are not enough; education requires experience. Experience generally refers to know-how or procedural knowledge (practical knowledge). The word *experience* aligns closely with the concept of experiment. A person with considerable experience in a specific field is called an expert. Experience could also refer to one's mental perception of events and subsequent reflection on or interpretation of these events. An experienced person has developed behavioral and communication skills, effective interpersonal relations, and integrity.

One accumulates experience over a period of time or from a single momentary event, such as a sudden change in environment. Mental experience involves the aspect of intellect and consciousness, which includes thought, perception, memory, willpower, learning, and imagination. Emotional experience in this context relates to the social skills of an individual that enable him or her to successfully participate and interact within society.

CHAPTER 5

Personality Disorders

Psychology

In the first four chapters, we explored the main components of personality. Those were: intelligence, emotional intelligence, social intelligence, and wisdom. They are the essential elements of psychology. In this chapter, we will continue demystifying psychology and get a feeling for what it is all about and discuss some common personality disorders. And in chapter 6, we will look at some mental health issues.

Psychology is the scientific study of behavior and experience—that is, the study of how human beings sense, think, learn, know, communicate, and interact. Modern psychology is devoted to collecting facts about behavior and experience and systematically organizing such facts into theories. These theories aid in understanding and explaining people's behavior and, sometimes, in predicting and influencing their future actions.

Historically, psychology has been divided into many interrelated subfields of study that frequently overlap. These are as follows:

- **Physiological** psychology is the study of, among other things, the functioning of the brain and nervous system and the role the secretion of hormones in the endocrine system plays in behavior.

- **Developmental** psychology is the study of the whole process of development, both physical and behavioral, from birth to death.

- **Social** psychology examines the ways in which people influence one another and the way they act in groups.

- **Industrial** psychology is the study of people's behavior at work and the effects of the work environment.

- **Educational** psychology diagnoses and treats those with learning difficulties and generally helps students make educational and career decisions.

- **Clinical** psychology assists those who have problems in daily life or who are mentally ill.

Psychology developed from many sources, but its origins as a science may be traced to ancient Greece, where it was originally a branch of philosophy. Plato and Aristotle, as well as other Greek philosophers, took up and studied some of psychology's basic questions regarding whether people are born with certain skills, abilities, and personalities or whether these develop as a result of experience. They researched how people develop and how they become so different from one another. Many questions relating to psychology were debated for centuries, but the roots of modern psychological theory can be found in the seventeenth century in the works of the French philosopher René Descartes and British philosophers Thomas Hobbes and John Locke.

Descartes argued that people's bodies are like clockwork machines, but that their minds are separate and unique. He maintained that minds have certain inborn ideas and that these ideas are crucial in organizing people's experience of the world. Hobbes and Locke, on the other hand, stressed the role of experience in the acquisition of human knowledge. Locke believed that all information about the physical world comes through the senses and that all correct ideas can be traced to the sensory information on which they are based.

Much of modern psychology developed along the lines of Locke's view. Some European psychologists who studied perception, however, held on to **Descartes's*** idea that some mental organization is natural; in fact, this concept still plays a role in contemporary theories of perception (thinking) and cognition (reasoning). It is seen in Noam Chomsky's theory of language and in Carl Jung's more speculative theory of personality. More generally, current research is revealing in detail how much nature—as compared to nurture—contributes to the causes of behavior.

** **René Descartes** (1596–1650) was a French philosopher, mathematician, and writer, today considered the father of modern and Western philosophies. He is well known for the philosophical statement, "I think, therefore I am." This statement is based on his conclusion that he can be certain that he exists because he thinks. He defined thought as "what happens in me such that I am immediately conscious of it, insofar as I am conscious of it." Thinking is thus every activity of a person of which the person is immediately conscious.*

Common Personality Disorders

The exact causes of personality disorders are not known. There are many confusing theories and assumptions as to whether they are learned or inherited. Likely it's a combination of the two, but the problem is in knowing how much may be due to inherited characteristics and how much may be learned. Anxiety, depression, and violence all seem to run in families, but this is not certain, and it is very hard to prove.

Research done mainly in the United States suggests that serious personality disorders, such as psychopathic tendencies, may be linked to a brain abnormality. The cause of the abnormality is also disputed: while some believe it is genetic, others think it is the result of an injury sustained during birth, infancy, or childhood.

However, there is consensus that most personality disorders are to some extent the result of a child's upbringing. In combination with the child's hereditary traits, negative and positive scenarios (depending on the child's perception) have a major impact on a child's psychology and the formation of his or her personality. The variance of impact on personality is directly related to the conditioning and the genetic makeup of a person, both of which determine his or her temperament, analytical power, and comprehension capacity.

Abnormal personality development probably results from a distortion in the interaction between the growing child and its environment. If, for example, a child has a problem with learning, problem solving, or emotional control, this not only affects the way he or she behaves, but it may also cause other people to respond negatively. As a result, the child comes to expect the worst from the world and thus tends to behave in a way that actually makes hostility and rejection more likely. So develops a vicious circle that, if it continues over years, distorts the child's psychological development.

Behaviorist B. F. Skinner described a process in which learning could occur through reinforcement and punishment. The process, known as **operant conditioning**, * functions by forming an association between a behavior and the consequences of the behavior. Skinner discovered that the timing of rewards and punishments has an important influence on how quickly a new behavior is acquired and the strength of the response.

Operant conditioning: B. F. Skinner, in 1938, coined the term operant conditioning; it means, roughly, changing behavior by the use of reinforcement, which is given after the desired response. His work was based *on Edward Thorndike's law of effect, but Skinner introduced a new term into the law: reinforcement. Behavior is reinforced (strengthened) by repetition, and if it is not reinforced, it tends to weaken or be extinguished.*

Skinner *(1904–1990) was an American psychologist, behaviorist, author, inventor, and social philosopher. He was a professor of psychology at Harvard University from 1958 until his retirement in 1974.*

Another recent study by the Centre for Emotional Health at Sydney's Macquarie University discovered that parents' control of their emotions could be the key to preventing mental illness in their children. Professor Ron Rapee's study found that treating the parents of very shy girls (as young as the age of three) could help prevent these girls from developing depression and anxiety in their teenage years. The major risks for severe shyness developing into anxiety or depression in later life appeared to be overprotection and overinvolvement of parents, as well as harsh and critical parenting. Professor Rapee said, "We were teaching parents different strategies to try to build confidence in their children." He added, "The girls, who were about three years old when the study started, were 15 percent less likely to develop an anxiety disorder by their teenage years if their parents were given the treatment. Almost none developed depression, compared to about 16 percent of the untreated girls."

Later in life, curing psychological problems starts with an individual's own efforts or with help from a qualified therapist. Identifying the problem is the first step in the process of bringing out into the conscious mind the causes that are buried deep in the subconscious. This allows the easily triggered emotional circuits to be the subject of relearning. An emotionally intelligent person, by digging deep into his or her subconscious, can begin the process on his or her own; others may need qualified help. Emotional circuits or complexes are formed either gradually as one grows up or suddenly as a result of a traumatic experience. Insecurity for example, develops gradually, but feelings of fear and panic could be the result of a single action, such as attempted rape, a dog attack, attempted murder, and so on.

Behavioral self-assessment depends on the person's own psychological energy, knowledge, and experience; these factors enable a person to discover personality disorders and complexes he or she has developed since birth. This entails going deep into one's subconscious to discover the causes of the negative behavior and learning how to eliminate, live with, or control them. With additional studies and experience, self-awareness could become the key to the ability of observing and assessing others. A disciplined personal response—the ability to control one's impulses in a range of situations and experiences—is essential to successful human relations. The formation of impulses and personality, except for the hereditary elements, normally starts from the day of birth, when the first contact is made with the external world. Behavioral conditioning to control the impulses also commences immediately after birth, when parents, nurses, friends, relatives, and caregivers try to ensure the child's adaptation to the external environment and conditioning toward social conformity. This is when the conflict between genetics and conditioning begins, as well as the formation of the conscious, the subconscious, the ego, and the superego.

In an adult, the ego could be manifested in the projected image of the person, while the superego is usually manifested in one's level of selfishness and narcissism. Ego and superego also relate to the person's feelings of insecurity or the inferiority complex, expressed in the level of narcissism. (For more on narcissism, see below.)

Intelligent conditioning depends on the person's inherited or learned brilliance. It is the ability to analyze and apply skills when dealing with others, which stems from thinking and learning. Knowledge and experience combined with the genetic makeup of a person are the main components of the person's perceived image. It should be emphasized that one's perceived image could be completely different from his or her projected image and self-image. The projected image is often a false image that is caused by one's mental distortion, which is aimed at deceiving the perceiver. (For more on self-image, see below.)

Psychological treatment aims to correct mental distortion by helping people to understand their problems and the reasons for their behaviors. Such treatment involves the patient's not only reaching this understanding but also relearning how to relate to others. Both psychotherapy and cognitive behavioral treatments can be helpful methods. Psychotherapy attempts to look at the way in which the person's earliest experiences have contributed to his or her problems. Cognitive behavioral treatment is more concerned with the here and now and tries to encourage the patient to learn new, more effective ways of thinking and behaving.

Cognitive therapists, psychoanalysts, and behavioral therapists are also occupied with solving the problems of depression, stress, and anxiety that have a negative effect on the general health of people. Overcoming these problems can improve productivity and reduce the nation's health care costs. Unfortunately, the medical establishment is not equipped to deal with the psychological aspects of medicine that can speed up patients' recovery. Also, as discussed earlier, teachers are not well trained in the basics of developmental psychology and emotional intelligence to be good mentors for children.

Research on depression has shown that depressed people often have inaccurate or faulty thoughts and beliefs about themselves, their situation, and the world. Once these inaccurate beliefs have been corrected, the person's perception of events and emotional state improve. According to cognitive therapy theory, how you feel is determined by what you think. Often, psychotherapy is the solution to depression and many other anxiety problems, especially when a person is having difficulty dealing with life and is in a great deal of anguish and mental pain.

The majority of mental disorders are caused by a dysfunctional communication pattern within the family, the school, or the workplace that can be corrected by cognitive therapy. The best solution, however, is for parents and schoolteachers to learn self-awareness and awareness of others to help children to grow and equip them with EI and SI. Behavioral psychology is not very complicated; it is based on rewards and punishments. For teenagers and adults, an effective and lasting change in behavior comes about by combining the understanding of behavioral psychology with other proven psychological techniques.

Dealing with depression and mental stress is extremely important for one's general health. A recent medical discovery found that depression, mental stress, and anxiety lower the body's immune response. Stress, anxiety, and depression are known to cause negative effects on the heart and stomach, contribute to conditions such as asthma and diabetes, increase vulnerability to viral infections, and speed up the spread of cancer. Many studies have found compelling evidence of their adverse effects on ill people as well. In particular, they impede recovery. On the other hand, positive emotions have a complementary effect on medical treatment. In other words, positive thinking and optimism are good armor for survival. Optimists generally make more efforts in their recovery and their well-being than pessimists, who generally lose hope easily and surrender to their negative emotions. Pessimists are more susceptible to the feeling of giving up hope. Accordingly, it can be concluded that emotional intelligence plays a major role in the health of individuals and the nation's health care cost.

In their book *Mental Disorders in Older Adults: Fundamentals of Assessment and Treatment,* (2011), Dr. Steven H. Zarit and Dr. Judy M. Zarit provide knowledge and skills for effective mental health practice with older adults. They demonstrate how to evaluate and treat frequently encountered clinical problems in this group, including mood and anxiety disorders and paranoid symptoms. Although the book deals with clinical problems of the aging population, many aspects of the book are applicable to other clinical psychology practices. It blends clinical expertise with research and provides guidance in assessment and intervention. It focuses on function rather than disease and emphasizes the importance of respecting the individual. As such, it contributes greatly to the field of mental health and aging.

Self-Image

Self-image is a mental picture or self-portrait or the way we see ourselves. It is the mental image that describes one's tangible and intangible characteristics, in both credit and liability, such as intelligence, talent, kindness, selfishness, beauty, or ugliness. Self-image is a product of learning from parents, school, colleagues, and friends. The strengths and weaknesses, including confidence and shyness, we learn when we are children affect our behavior in adulthood. One's self-portrait is important because it affects how the person thinks and feels about his or her personality and how he or she relates to others, which affects the quality of interpersonal relationships. A positive self-image leads to positive emotional and social intelligences. A negative self-image, which focuses on faults, weaknesses, failures, and imperfections, leads to the opposite.

Although self-image appears to be resistant to change, it is always subject to change in direct relation to our dynamic mental capacity and the way we analyze and adapt to events. In life we learn that our self-image can be distorted by our perceived image. The perceived image of a person is the outcome of the psychology of the perceiver, which influences how he or she sees the individual. Thus, self-image is also the result of the individual's perception of the way others see him or her.

One's projected image, on the other hand, is an artificial self-portrait based on a module that may also be distorted by misreading of our social settings. For example, taking oneself too seriously and projecting a pompous or self-important image is an attempt to distort others' perceptions about oneself. Such distortion can lead to problems like the delusion of superiority, paranoia, and obsession. Often this sort of image is exposed as phony and rejected by the immediate social circle, which causes the person to become withdrawn and burdened with the feeling of isolation.

Consistent projection of a false image is a personality disorder related to insecurity or lack of self-esteem. This can be observed through the behavior of the sufferer: it's when the person listens to his or her own voice only, forming a single person's political or social party within, and constantly seeks self-promotion and attention—often at the expense of others. When self-promotion is at the expense of others, it becomes part of an unhealthy form of narcissism. (For more on unhealthy narcissism, see below.) A phony projected image can be detected when the sufferer doesn't have substance when intentionally criticizing others. Often during a conversation, if somebody deservedly gets praised for something, the sufferer may directly or indirectly convey a message that he or she is worthy of the same or even better. Self-promotion also takes the form of dismissing others' worthy achievements without knowing the details or the facts of these achievements. It could also manifest itself in the sufferer's unreasonable criticism and demeaning of others for the sake of making himself or herself appear to be a standout. Self-promotion at the expense of others and the constant desire to be favorably compared to others are common problems associated with a phony projected image. Persistent projection of a false image, especially in the absence of backup substance, is a recipe for a personality disorder that could be caused by the feeling of insecurity or inferiority. (For more on insecurity and inferiority, see below.)

To avoid the pitfalls of a false image, one must act realistically, be a true self, and not worry about how others perceive him or her. To overcome the problem, it is necessary to develop self-awareness to control the distortion. The individual must not attempt to compare himself or herself to others and must attempt to be modest (modesty is a virtue), to develop positive thinking, and to be constructive.

To restore one's positive self-image, it is essential to avoid comparing oneself favorably to others by stereotyping, derogating, discriminating, or expressing bigotry and prejudice. Above all, it is essential to have self-confidence. And finally, having a positive self-image is not attempting to be a perfectionist; such a person sets a standard for success above the norms of achievable goals, which makes him or her more prone to having a negative self-image (as a result of exposure to failure and disappointment).

Narcissism

Beyond its natural healthy form, narcissism becomes an unhealthy antisocial personality disorder that often leads to violating the rights of others. The term *narcissism*, in keeping with the Greek myth of Narcissus, refers to self-love. It's a person's preoccupation with self and his or her needs, and how he or she is perceived by others. It's a mental state in which there is self-worship and excessive interest in one's own perfection. People with unhealthy narcissistic personalities tend to be self-important and to need constant attention and admiration, which basically means that a person is totally absorbed in the self. Such a person's behaviors include wanting excessively to please others, being unable to empathize with others, having little interest in close relationships, and having the feeling of being entitled to special treatment. The symptoms are worse when narcissism is based on an underlying low sense of self-esteem. Although a person with a narcissistic personality disorder has an exaggerated sense of superiority, this usually hides insecurity and an inferiority complex.

Many mental health professionals observe that narcissism is the result of parenting extremes. Overpampering a child or pushing others to recognize a child as special could cause the problem. Or it could be the result of neglect or an abusive upbringing. The symptoms of narcissism as a personality disorder usually appear in early adulthood. Teenagers may exhibit narcissistic traits, like seeking attention and admiration, but they usually outgrow these traits by early adulthood if they develop emotional intelligence.

> **Warning:** The following four paragraphs could be a bit tedious and confusing to some readers. When you feel so inclined, please skip to the section on forms of narcissism below.

The notion of narcissism was proposed by Freud in the early twentieth century, based on the term borrowed from Paul Nacke, who in 1899 described a form of behavior resembling a perversion, whereby an individual treated his or her own body as one might treat the body of a sexual partner. In a case study, Freud offered this explanation: "There comes a time in the development of the individual at which he unifies his sexual instincts (which have hitherto been engaged in auto-erotic activities) in order to obtain a love-object; and he begins by taking himself, his own body as his love-object." Freud thus formed the hypothesis of a narcissistic stage of development occurring between the auto-erotic stage and the stage of object-love. In his book *Instincts and Their Vicissitudes*, (1915), he described the primal psychological situation as follows: "Originally, at the very beginning of mental life, the ego is part of instincts. And to some extent, ego is capable of satisfying instincts on its own." He called this condition "narcissism," which is the way to obtaining satisfaction, or auto-eroticism.

On the other hand, Andre Green in his book, *Life Narcissism, Death Narcissism*, (2001), saw the conflict surrounding the relationship differently. He concluded that because narcissism affords the ego a certain degree of independence by transferring the desire of the "Other to the desire of the One," a lethal kind of narcissism must be considered, for the object is destroyed at the beginning of this process. Rather than unpleasure, it is the "neutral" that replaces pleasure. In this connection, Green says that Freud had proposed the metaphor of the return to the inanimate (spiritless and pulseless). As for Freud's analysis of masochism (getting pleasure from self-inflicted pain), which distinguished between erogenous (sensitive to sexual stimulation) masochism, female masochism, and moral masochism, Green suggested physical narcissism, intellectual narcissism, and moral narcissism, without suggesting any analogy between his and Freud's terms. It appears that beyond these intellectual suppositions, there is not much to learn, other than a philosophical or a semantic argument.

From this point onward, **Freud**, * his theories, and the associated technical terminology he uses become even more complicated, and they are of little benefit to the general reader. Due to the heavy use of metaphors and scientific and technical terms often not found in a common dictionary, the works of some psychologists become burdensome and hard to comprehend. Many modern psychologists, however, are aware of this problem and avoid using heavy technical and philosophical terms. Some other modern psychologists still (maybe unintentionally) tend to jumble a scientific approach with metaphors without attempting to clarify their thoughts. For instance, they often use the term *heart* to refer to a thinking object even though the heart is actually a mechanical organ for pumping blood.

Freud: *Sigismund Schlomo Freud (1856–1939) was an Austrian neurologist who became known as the founding father of psychoanalysis. After he became a doctor of medicine at the University of Vienna in 1881, he carried out research into cerebral palsy, aphasia (inability to use or understand language because of brain injury), and microscopic neuroanatomy at Vienna General Hospital. He was appointed a university lecturer in neuropathology in 1885, and he became a professor in 1902. He developed therapeutic techniques, including free association, in which patients report their thoughts without reservation and in the order they spontaneously occur, and discovered transference, in which patients declare the feelings derived from the sexual experiences and fantasies of their childhood, establishing these feelings as central in the analytical process. In 1899, he developed his theories about the unconscious in The Interpretation of Dreams.*

Forms of Narcissism

Some forms of narcissism that relate to the normal ego are healthy and natural; they enable a person to take responsibility for and take care of himself or herself without affecting others negatively. Beyond this, narcissism becomes unhealthy or extreme and leads to emotional isolation, which may require professional treatment. Narcissism is common and has both a direct and indirect impact on our daily life and our interpersonal relationships.

It is not my intention here to analyze well-known events and megalomaniacs that the majority of readers are familiar with, such as Hitler and Stalin. Since the nineteenth century, extreme narcissism has been a subject well researched and explored by many psychologists and writers. Human history is rich with examples of leaders who were and are still afflicted with extreme narcissism that caused major conflicts and calamities—ranging from the world's financial crises to wars. Extreme narcissism afflicts only a small number of adults, but because of its complexity, it has been afforded more than a reasonable share of research by an army of writers and psychologists. My intention here is to throw more light on healthy and unhealthy forms of narcissism. Readers can relate to and understand these forms of narcissism by easily recognizing children and adults in their own immediate social environment that manifest the symptoms of healthy or unhealthy narcissism. Above all, understanding narcissism can help many readers to gain self-awareness.

Healthy Narcissism

Narcissism is normal if it provides one with a sense of self-esteem, ambition, and the capacity to form satisfying relationships. It's based on the principle of loving yourself as you are and then doing your best. As long as it can be integrated into one's normal mental health, then it is not toxic. Healthy and natural (instinctive) forms of narcissism belong to one or more of the following types: acquired situational, amorous, compensatory, and cross-cultural. The characteristics of this group range between fantasy, vanity, perfectionism, egotism, normal selfishness, true self, and normal greed. In healthy narcissism, the person understands that he or she is prone to making mistakes, and healthy narcissists are differentiated from unhealthy narcissists by their intellectual honesty to accept when they are smart, when they are lucky, and when they are wrong.

The narcissistic personality does not completely characterize the psychological quality of narcissism. Freud, for example, maintained that narcissism could be positive, especially in early child development, when the child needs to establish the foundation of self-love. In order to help the child establish a healthy personality, parents can help their children by providing the right balance between too much admiration and too little positive attention. Parents who lavish an undue amount of praise may lead the child to develop the delusion of grandeur, which is one of the forms of extreme narcissism called megalomania. (For more on megalomania, see "Extreme Narcissism" below.) The opposite approach can produce a child with the vulnerable form of narcissism in what is called the **psychodynamic mask model**. * Again, the application of the happy medium of not too little and not too much is the right approach. Generally, children start life with a modestly positive self-image, and with the right parental approach, they can carry the positive self-image into their adolescence. A healthy foundation to their personality can help them continue to adapt positively to life.

*** The psychodynamic mask model of narcissism** is one of the most influential perspectives concerning the dynamics of narcissism, derived from the models of narcissism offered by psychologists Kohut (1966) and Kernberg (1975). Both Kohut and Kernberg agree that the overt grandiosity of narcissists serves as a façade to conceal underlying feelings of inferiority and low self-esteem that are believed to stem from early experiences of inadequate and insensitive parenting. That is, the grandiosity expressed by narcissists is not believed to be completely authentic.*

According to researchers, a moderate amount of the right kind of narcissism can actually be beneficial to well-being. They have identified the quality of *adaptive narcissism*, which can give a person self-confidence that enables him or her to cope with anxiety and to assume leadership positions. They also have reasons to believe that having some adaptive narcissism helps a person to maintain healthy habits, including professionalism. This in turn increases the person's desire to set higher goals in life. A motivated person with high self-confidence is better able to find the balance between dependence and self-sufficiency in the role of a husband or a wife; in the role of a parent, he or she would rather see the children develop as individuals rather than dependents and conformists.

Jeremy Holmes from United Kingdom Freud Organization suggests that liking oneself is a precondition for liking others. Yet to be in love with oneself is at best suspect, at worst a tragic fate condemning the afflicted to a life deprived of true intimacy.

Narcissism is a universal psychological phenomenon, with healthy and unhealthy forms. Pathological forms of narcissism may be an attempt to find basic security in the face of environmental difficulty or trauma. Psychological treatment can help lessen the fundamental loneliness of the narcissistic sufferer.

To develop healthy narcissism, one should do the following:

- First, the person must become self-aware and realistic about the self and have a good understanding of others.

- Second is to be physically fit and healthy as part of developing self-confidence. Feeling good about oneself radiates through a person and improves his or her professional standing and interpersonal relationships. Having a sense of humor can help, too.

- Third is to develop sufficient knowledge to be in a position of control rather than becoming a blind follower and target of political and religious manipulation or indoctrination.

- Fourth, one should develop empathy for others because empathy is contagious and mutual.

- Fifth is to remember that a healthy narcissist always ensures that fulfilling his or her needs and attaining his or her freedom doesn't ever affect others' needs and freedom in an adverse way. Healthy narcissism is a constructive decision-making process.

- Sixth is to remember that an unhealthy narcissist is a master of violating boundaries and has no respect for others' emotional, mental, physical, or spiritual space. The best relationship to have with an unhealthy narcissist is no relationship, unless he or she has attained redemption.

- Seventh is to remember that healthy narcissism helps one discover personal weaknesses and enables him or her to convert them into strengths, provided he or she has integrated the healthy narcissism into his or her conscious mind. And it is about accepting oneself as he or she is and in doing his or her best.

Finally, if you did everything you could and still find yourself stuck, unhappy, or distressed, you should seek counseling.

The roots of unhealthy narcissism may be long-standing and deep, and counseling can help you find a needed balance between self-acceptance and overinflated ego and self-love.

Unhealthy Narcissism (also called toxic narcissism)

When a child is raised to believe that he or she is the center of the universe and is entitled to do and get anything he or she wants (spoiled rotten), that child is likely to become an unhealthy narcissist. Meeting the child's unrealistic expectations gives him or her an overinflated sense of self-love and self-worth coupled with the inability to differentiate right and wrong. This is in addition to overindulgence, excessive admiration, and overvaluation of the child by parents and caregivers, without attempting to balance the positives with the negatives. To overinflate the child's ego, it is common for parents to tell their child that he or she is the best or is at least better than other children. This unfortunately often happens when the parents themselves are unhealthy narcissists.

The major flaw with this sort of upbringing is that it ignores the child's inherited temperament and perception. As a result, the child doesn't develop the sense of equality and mutuality that is the key to successful human relations. Such a child most likely grows up having a feeling of excessive self-importance and superiority, takes advantage of others to achieve his or her own goals, is in need of constant attention and admiration, becomes excessively selfish, and becomes obsessed with vanity, prestige, and power. Such

a child has the potential to develop into an extreme narcissist. Furthermore, because of his or her unrealistic expectations, the child is unlikely to be able to cope with the ups
and downs of life, especially the downs. In many instances,
such a child will live with high anxiety that can lead
to depression.

Narcissism is not normal when it takes over a person's
every act and thought; at that point, it becomes a personality disorder. It makes the person act in toxic ways toward
others. An unhealthy narcissist uses many methods to protect himself or herself at the expense of others. He or she
tends to devalue, derogate, and blame others for any negative outcome. Although an unhealthy narcissist could be
ambitious and capable, he or she lacks the ability to toler-
ate setbacks, work cooperatively with others, or maintain
long-term professional achievements.

As a personality disorder, unhealthy narcissism
belongs to one or more of the following: aggressive, jealous, closet (hiding), extremely selfish, conversational,
and destructive. The characteristics of this group include
being insidious, calculating, boastful, arrogant, conceited,
pretentious, * untrustworthy, egocentric, intolerant of
others, envious, **manipulative**, ** opportunistic, and
superficial. Such individuals may lack empathy, project
a false image (false persona), aim to be compared favorably to others, promote the self at the expense of others,
and lack self-esteem, and have **success orientation.** ***
Their fragile self-esteem often drives them to belittle or
disparage others in their attempt to exaggerate their own

self-worth. Often, through jealousy and envy, they sabotage the positive image and the reputation of others for their self-promotion.

Afflicted people are usually in a state of denial or self-idealization, and they often adopt the strategy of distorting the facts. Some of the descriptions of an unhealthy narcissist overlap with the description of an extreme narcissist. Some narcissists may have the ability to change into a variety of personas according to the situation. Sometimes they may be intimidating; sometimes they may be pretending to be empathetic and charming.

* **Pretentious narcissists** are narcissists afflicted with delusions who pretend to be more than what they really are.

** **Manipulative narcissists** are narcissists who value only what works for them at the expense of others.

*** **Success-oriented narcissists** are narcissists who become close friends and keep you as a close friend as long as you are useful. Once they discover that you are too smart for their manipulative techniques, or when you do not have anything more to offer after they have taken all they needed to take from you, they abandon you.

Toxic narcissists are usually very critical of others to ensure that they always compare favorably. Because their aim is to always look better than others and to be the center of attention, they are often perceived as arrogant and superior. Toxic narcissists have no qualms about violating others' space, and when they succeed once, they can easily do it again and again.

Furthermore, a toxic narcissist doesn't have the same feeling of empathy that a normal person does; instead, the individual uses empathy to fulfill his or her needs at the expense of others. When unhealthy narcissists are discovered within their social circles, because of their obvious manipulation, they become burdensome and awkward to be with. A lesson to learn is not to be deceived by their appearance; they are obsessed with themselves and their needs and have little interest in being an equal partner or a friend.

Fortunately, however, a toxic narcissist can redeem himself or herself in the following ways:

- First, an unhealthy form of narcissism can be solved by digging deep into the subconscious to discover the causes of one's predicament. It could be driven by insecurity or an inferiority complex. Bringing the psychological disorder into the conscious mind, which can be achieved with basic knowledge of psychology, is a big step toward self-help. It can also help to discover the original trigger of the problem that could have been during childhood, which may have been caused by faulty parenting.

- Second is the attunement phase whereby the narcissist needs to have the courage to come out in the open and acknowledge his or her past and present behaviors and make a commitment to total redemption.

- Third, when the problem cannot be solved by self-help because it is deeply entrenched and persistent, professional help should be sought. Such help is more effective than medication, provided that the afflicted person is willing to go through self-reflection or a change of personality.

Accordingly, a relationship can be sustained with a narcissist, but the residual effect of past behaviors is difficult to erase unless his or her entire social circle becomes convinced that total redemption has been attained.

> **Confirming note:** Because narcissism occurs in different degrees, many of the characteristics of unhealthy narcissism overlap with the characteristics of extreme narcissism. Some the characteristics are more harmful than others, especially when the problem is deeply entrenched and cannot be solved without professional help. The problem is aggravated by the fact that all his or her life, the afflicted person has been the master of hiding and denial, even to himself or herself. Counseling will achieve nothing if the narcissist is not committed or not willing to be cured, especially when the cure entails opening old wounds.

Extreme Narcissism

Extreme narcissism is the ultimate destructive form of narcissism in which the afflicted person embarks on using and exploiting others at any presented opportunity. It is an obsessive-compulsive personality disorder characterized by a preoccupation with mental and interpersonal control at the expense of flexibility and openness. This entrenched personality disorder can be described as the feeling of grandiosity—either based in fantasy or reflected in the actual behavior. It can develop into psychopathic mental illness. An expert on narcissism, Otto Kernberg, views psychopathy as the most severe, most extreme, and most malignant form of narcissism. In his book *Borderline Conditions and Pathological Narcissism*, (1992), wrote:

> Psychopaths have most severe difficulties in all the above three areas of (most severe, most extreme, and most malignant). They protect their self-esteem through immoral or violent behavior, are characterized by intense rage and envy, and tend to be irritable and to exploit others. They engage in immoral, violent, or criminal behavior, are revengeful and sadistic, and lack any sense of guilt or remorse.

Generally, for an extreme narcissist, people or friends are there for him or her to use. The afflicted person is always in need of admiration. Driven by a belief in their primary importance, extreme narcissists usually have a complete lack of empathy toward others. They often display snobbishness, disdain, or a patronizing attitude toward others.

Many researchers believe that the afflicted person must be at least eighteen years old before extreme narcissism can be diagnosed. It occurs in less than 1 percent of the general population and appears to be more common in males than females. Like most personality disorders, it typically decreases in intensity with age. A person afflicted with a severe form of such a personality disorder usually doesn't seek treatment until the disorder starts to interfere with or drastically affect his or her life. Treatment of the severe form of the disorder involves long-duration psychotherapy and may also involve medication when there are specific threatening symptoms.

At the core of extreme narcissism is an egotistical preoccupation with the self, personal preferences, aspirations, and needs. The individual will be pompous, obsessed with success at all costs, and overly concerned with the way he or she is perceived by others.

The culmination of major emotional traumas goes back to childhood, which eventually causes the afflicted person to become dysfunctional, despised, and rejected. An extreme narcissist tends to cut others off, eventually becoming emotionally isolated. The extreme narcissist is emotionally stuck at the inception of the suffering that could be hereditary or caused by unsuitable parenting or major trauma, and no matter how socially skilled he or she later becomes, this person will have emotional dysfunction, especially the general feeling that people are harmful and cannot be trusted, which culminates in adopting a false image to suit his or her perceived social environment. An extreme narcissist is usually reluctant to delegate tasks or to work with others unless they do things exactly his or her way.

Some narcissists may develop the ability to change into different identities to suit the occasion; they may become scary, tough, and intimidating, or they may become a nice and caring person whom everyone likes and wants to be with.

When an extreme or an unhealthy narcissist realizes that he or she cannot control or exploit you, this person will drop you or avoid you like the plague. He or she will also avoid you if you have a more powerful image than he or she does. As for reciprocal loyalty, you shouldn't expect any from an extreme or unhealthy narcissist.

Extreme narcissism belongs to one or more of the following types: egomaniac, elitist, fanatical, malignant, megalomaniac, pathological, and unprincipled. The characteristics of this group include exploitation, grandiosity, grandstanding, excessive greed, hidden agendas, rage, self-absorption, self-righteousness, superiority complexes, and megalomania. **Megalomania*** is commonly understood as a mental behavior characterized by an excessive desire for power and glory and by illusory feelings of having infinite power and greatness. It's a product of the superego and the pinnacle of extreme narcissism. Some aspects of the destructive nature of megalomania are described in my book Thorny Opinion, (2008).

__Megalomania:__ The delusion of grandeur is a form of paranoid schizo-phrenia. It comprises the superego and overconfidence, but its under-current is fear and the feeling of inferiority. It can be a characteristic of power-drunk or control-freak dictators, some executives, some politi-cians, and some army generals. It can be a hereditary mental illness or an acquired personality disorder. It develops gradually if it is a personality disorder and suddenly if it is hereditary. The afflicted person might require psychiatric treatment and medication if the conditions are severe, espe-cially when the sufferer displays an obvious exaggeration of self-worth, aggression, impulsiveness, obsession, mood swings, paranoia, vengeful-ness, cruelty, and so on. People with these characteristics usually are anti-social, vengeful, violent, and suspicious of people around them.

A milder form of megalomania could affect some people in power, espe-cially the obsessive moral-crusading politicians and people who show signs of aggression and ruthlessness toward others. This can be observed when politicians display the desire to destroy their opponents by sarcasm, rude-ness, bullying, arrogance, degradation, character assassination, and so on.

An extreme narcissist is usually the center of his or her own universe and tends to be the one who moves toward cutting others off and eventually becoming emotionally isolated. To an extreme narcissist, people are things to be used. The disorder usually starts with a significant emo-tional wound or a series of them culminating in a major trauma of separation or attachment. Because an extreme narcissist is frozen in childhood, no matter how socially skilled the person becomes, he or she continues to be dysfunctional. And as stated earlier, an extreme narcissist is the master of covering up and hiding, even to himself or herself.

After many years of teaching himself or herself to be disconnected from his or her own feelings, the extreme narcissist tends to live in the realm of his or her own reasons—a realm the individual feels he or she can control. The extreme narcissist's realm is devoid of feelings that become unsafe to the narcissist and the people around him or her.

Finally, the extreme narcissist becomes destructive and dangerous to himself or herself, friends, and society. Some extreme narcissists differ from other narcissists in the fact that they desire to be powerful rather than charming and strive to be feared rather than loved. Hitler was one of those extreme pathological narcissists.

> **Note:** As insecurity and inferiority relate to unhealthy and extreme narcissism, respectively, and as there are some common threads between them, there are some common threads between insecurity and inferiority. (See below.)

Insecurity

Emotional insecurity is a general feeling of anxiety that may be caused by an individual's perception of being vulnerable and unstable, which affects his or her self-image or ego. It is the opposite of emotional security, or the stability of an individual's emotional state. Emotional security relates to the

individual's psychological resilience. A person who is emotionally secure is not susceptible to setbacks or depressions,
and his or her peace of mind is not threatened by even a
major disturbance. Vulnerability and instability and, thus, an
insecure individual, are easy to spot: his or her views, opinions, and ideas are shaped by others because he or she is
uncertain about his or her ability to stand up and be counted.

Insecurity affects different people in many different
ways, and to a **different degree**, * which is usually relative
to the person's own perception of himself or herself. To a
certain extent, observing and understanding the insecurities of others may help you discover and understand your
own problems, but it's more important to understand your
own insecurities before attempting to find the same in
others. Discovering your own problems can help you find a
way to get along with people instead of feeling threatened
by them and will allow you to ward off any toxic thoughts
and behaviors. It can also help you find your own values
instead of constantly trying to please people or blindly following their points of view and perceptions. The people
you want to please in order to be accepted in their social
circle could be narcissistic, manipulative, and uncompro-
mising. Such people may try to exploit others' weaknesses
and are quick to identify and prey on the insecure. When
you recognize signs of such negative qualities, you should
be alert and exercise care about what you do and how you
behave. Let them know where you stand to make it harder
for them to abuse your presence. Above all, when another's insecurity is clear and open to exploitation, you should

never attempt to take advantage of such vulnerability. As a wise person, it is your responsibility to create harmonious relationships.

> *** Different degree:** It is a well established fact that the majority of people are emotionally vulnerable and capable of being hurt, which implies that emotional insecurity and its management are relative to an individual's emotional intelligence or self-awareness. The degree to which vulnerability is entrenched equals the degree of power it has on the life of each individual. In the absence of the mental power of compensation, insecurity may contribute to the development of an inferiority complex, shyness, paranoia, and social withdrawal.

Insecure individuals usually lack confidence in their own value and capacity because of a lack of trust in themselves or others. **Abraham Maslow**** describes an insecure person as a person who "perceives the world as a threatening jungle and most human beings as dangerous and selfish; feels rejected and isolated, anxious and hostile; is generally pessimistic and unhappy; shows signs of tension and conflict; tends to turn inward; is troubled by guilt-feelings; has one or another disturbance of self-esteem; tends to be neurotic; and is generally selfish and egocentric."

*** Abraham Maslow** *(1908–1970) was an American psychology professor at Brandeis University and Columbia University. He was concerned
with the question of people's self-actualization or if their basic needs
are met. He was a humanistic psychologist who believed that everybody
has the desire to realize his or her full potential to reach a level of self-
actualization. He believed that self-actualized people can have many
peak experiences throughout a day while other people have fewer of
these experiences. Self-actualizing people tend to focus on problems
outside themselves, have a clear sense of what is true and what is false,
are spontaneous and creative, and are not bound too strictly by social
conventions.*

As discussed earlier, emotional intelligence—especially
the ability to observe and understand the relationship
between one's responses and their triggers—is the key to
behavioral modification. Insecurity is the most universally
common psychological disorder and possibly the easiest of
all the disorders to resolve through self-awareness, determination, mental energy, and self-analysis. This in itself
could be the major step toward understanding others who
share the same social and work environments. In many
situations, the experience gained in a particular environment and the ensuing self-assessment made could result
in behavioral modification that may be applied to achieve
better outcomes in any new environment. Insecurity can
be resolved by patience and realization that an individual's
value depends on his or her perspective or the subjective
opinion of oneself. (An individual's subjective opinion usually relates to his or her own reality, which doesn't mean

that he or she is comfortable in his or her own social environment.)

The common characteristics of insecurity are feelings of inadequacy, lack of courage to face problems, jealousy, low spirits, envy, sensitivity, incompetency, inability to win, inability to achieve recognition and respect, undue pessimism, gossiping, lack of sense of humor, often feeling misunderstood, lack of confidence, lack of trust, aimlessness, inability to relate to others, inability to meet expectations, feelings of rejection, and constant need of compliments and reassurance.

To cover up the symptoms, the sufferer might behave subconsciously by being defensive (often turns defense into an attack), displaying arrogance, displaying a "me too" syndrome, shifting blame onto others, taking credit for everything, being highly judgmental, pretending to know everything, pretending to be more intelligent than and superior to others, being dismissive of others, constantly bragging and self-praising, denying responsibility, and trying to make a name for himself or herself at the expense of others.

The sufferer could have one or more of the above feelings and symptoms and may attempt to hide the symptoms by one or more of the above methods. Most of the above feelings and symptoms are also common characteristics of unhealthy narcissism.

The general causes of insecurity are feeling excessively self-conscious, giving in to peer pressure, being bullied, not being accepted or being rejected by others, facing unrealistically high expectations from parents and schools, experiencing major trauma, having a negative body image, living in an unsuitable environment, lacking skills or guidance, being constantly ridiculed by others or overshadowed by siblings, and, most importantly, lacking motivation in the early stages of development. Other causes may relate to an experience of domestic verbal or emotional abuse, physical or sexual abuse, bullying at school or in the workplace, and so on. The victims will develop defense mechanisms to protect their poorly formed egos that are diminished by the domination of others who are in a position of power over them.

Parents and the home environment are the most likely causes of the formulation of personality disorders, especially when considering that the parents' own egos and insecurities might have an immediate reflection on their children.

Some parents' egos could have been directed toward convincing their child that he or she is the best or at least that he or she is better than the others. This might seem a natural thing to do in building the child's self-esteem, but at the same time, it could be perceived as a high expectation, one that the child feels unable to meet. Convincing the child that he or she is the best can create either the delusion of really being the best or the feeling of surrender when he or she cannot meet the parents' expectation, especially the child who is subjected to constant ridicule and bullying. In the absence of corrective measures, the child who is laden with the delusion of being the best could later in life become a bully or dismissive of others or a know-it-all. He or she will likely be obsessive, aggressive, defensive, snobbish, and so on. On the other hand, the child who is laden with the feeling of surrender could later in life display feelings of inadequacy, isolation, low spirits, an inability to relate to others, and incompetency and may become the target of bullying. In both instances, a trauma could persist until it is dealt with. The trauma could lead to a false and conflicting self-image and, in a severe case, could become deeply entrenched as mental illness, which might require professional help.

The entrenchment into the subconscious of an insecurity disorder could be further aggravated by subjecting the child to very rigid expectations and by inadequate psychological reinforcement provided by parents and at school, which is the direct result of deficient methods of teaching. The consequences of a low standard of education and poor social and personal development are more personality disorders and more antisocial behavior.

To overcome insecurity one can take several steps:

- First is to recognize the existence of the problem. The earlier the discovery of the problem, the easier it is to resolve. The more time that passes, the more entrenched it becomes in the subconscious.

- Second is developing self-belief and the understanding that nobody is perfect.

- Third is understanding that life is full of ups and downs and learning to grapple and live with this reality.

- Fourth is learning *not* to be critical of others and *not* to judge them by the way they fall, but by the way they get up—the same treatment one would want for himself or herself.

- Fifth is developing general knowledge and a sense of humor, two necessary ingredients for interpersonal relationships, social interaction, and mental comfort.

- Finally, talking to a trustworthy person about the problem might lead to a useful outcome.

Inferiority Complex

An inferiority complex is a personality disorder that stems from the conflict between the desire to be noticed and the fear of being humiliated. It is characterized by aggressiveness and inflated self-confidence or by withdrawal into oneself and lack of self-esteem or self-confidence. While these may seem to be at odds with one another, researchers found that a persistent sense of inadequacy or a tendency to self-diminishment sometimes results in excessive aggressiveness through **overcompensation**. * The term *inferiority complex* was coined to indicate a lack of covert self-esteem. For many, it is developed through genetic personality characteristics and environmental factors, such as homelife, school, work, or other personal experiences.

*** Overcompensation** *is the attempt to overcome a real or imagined defect or unwanted trait by overly exaggerating its opposite.*

Inferiority complex is a term sometimes used to describe the behavior of a person who compensates for his or her feelings of inferiority—feeling like he or she is less than others, not as good as others, worthless, and so on—by acting in ways that make him or her appear superior and sometimes snobbish. Such individuals do this because controlling others' perceptions helps them feel less inadequate. An inferiority complex may cause an individual to overcompensate for his or her weaknesses. For example, when someone feels inferior because he or she is shorter than average, the person may become overly concerned with his or her body image. He or she may go on a strict diet or engage in rigorous exercise, hoping that a slimmer body will make him or her appear taller. If concern over body image is taken to the extreme, it can develop into neurosis, paranoia, or anorexia. (For more on body image, see below.)

Anyone in the world—big or small, fat or thin, black or white—can feel inferior at times. We tell ourselves that we aren't good enough, pretty enough, or smart enough, yet these comments are in no way based on facts.

Generally speaking, feeling inferior is caused by multiple factors that gradually build themselves into a person's character. The results of verbal, physical, and emotional abuse can have long-lasting, psychologically damaging effects on a person, making him or her believe that he or she is less deserving of acceptance. An inferiority complex can also be described as a persistent feeling of being inferior to others in some way. It is usually connected to a real or imaginary shortcoming in physical appearance, intelligence, personality, education, social status, or economic status.

The afflicted person will be passive, pessimistic, shy, and overly apologetic. These behaviors are the result of the emotions typical of an inferiority complex: feelings of diminished self-worth and increased doubt and uncertainty, as well as feelings of shame, humiliation, and rejection and a sense of not measuring up to society's standards. An inferiority complex is often subconscious, and it is thought to drive an afflicted individual to overcompensate, resulting in either spectacular achievement or extreme antisocial behavior. Depending on his or her perception, a person with an inferiority complex will either succumb to it or use it as an incentive to excel. People who succumb to an inferiority complex could become a burden on society by being useless, aggressive, antisocial, and rebellious. In addition, they could turn to crime. These people could also have a negative impact on national productivity.

The feeling of inadequacy is usually triggered and entrenched in children when they are constantly criticized, put down, discouraged, and embarrassed by parents, friends, and teachers.

In some instances, it could become aggravated by general ignorance of motivational methods in the country's education system. It could also be cultural. The cultural element here is not meant to stereotype people from specific backgrounds; it applies only to people with inferiority disorders from all cultural backgrounds. It could manifest itself, for example, in a group that tends to cut down others (the tall poppy syndrome) or in the tendency of the inadequate person to assume that other people of the same cultural background are equally inadequate. A person from a different country who is afflicted with an inferiority complex tends to dismiss his or her own culture as inferior to the culture of other countries. Also, the afflicted person tends to dismiss anybody that relates to him or her as inferior, including his or her own family and siblings. An inferiority complex is often linked to the display of anti-intellectual attitudes toward thinkers, scientists, and other achievers of one's original country. These tendencies are prevalent in individuals coming from postcolonial nations, as colonial powers thrived on destroying the spirit of the colonized.

No matter his or her background, an afflicted individual sometimes places blame on race, gender, genetics, sexual orientation, family, social class, mental health, physical appearance, or any character trait that he or she feels is lacking.

According to Alfred Adler, (1912), a feeling of inferiority may be brought about by one's upbringing (e.g., being compared to a sibling), experiences of social discrimination (e.g., having limited opportunities due to race, economic situation, or gender), or having physical and mental limitations. Classical **Adlerian psychology*** makes a distinction between primary and secondary inferiority feelings:

- A primary inferiority feeling is said to be rooted in one's original childhood experience of weakness, helplessness, and dependency. It can then be intensified by comparisons to siblings, romantic partners, and other adults.

- A secondary inferiority feeling relates to an adult's experience of being unable to reach a subconscious fictional final goal of subjective security and success to compensate for feelings of inferiority. The perceived distance from that goal would lead to a negative or depressed feeling that could then prompt the recall of the original inferiority feeling; this composite of inferiority feelings could be experienced as overwhelming. The goal invented to relieve the original, primary feeling of inferiority actually causes the secondary feeling of inferiority in such individuals; it is a Catch-22. This vicious circle is common in neurotic lifestyles.

* **Adlerian psychology** was first developed by **Alfred Adler**** and is based on the importance of perceptions and social relationships to the emotional and physical health of families and communities. Adler believed that the health of families, classrooms, workplaces, and so on relies heavily on mutual respect and equality. He also believed that human *beings are goal-oriented and choice-making by nature, not mechanistic victims of instincts, drives, and the environment. Humans respond to reality according to their private logic—not as it is, but rather as they perceive it to be. As social beings, humans' basic goal is to belong. Although heredity and environment have strong influences, to a large extent the person makes his or her own choices of how to belong. Adlerian psychology has a strong focus on prevention of mental disturbance and social distress through education and parenting.*

*** **Alfred Adler**, MD (1870–1937) was a Viennese physician and founder of Adlerian psychology. Much of his work was with teachers and parents who wanted to replace traditional authoritarian styles of relating to children with more democratic, but not permissive, ways. Many schools incorporate his methods in teacher training and classroom work, including many parenting courses. He is famous for identifying the inferiority complex, life tasks, and social interest. His philosophy is humanistic, optimistic, and pragmatic. One of his popular sayings was, "We do not always have control over what happens to us, but we can, and do, decide how to respond to what occurs. We are responsible for our choices and actions. We can change and grow. We may not be aware of making choices or of the consequences of our choices, but we are responsible for them. Life deals the cards, we play the hand."*

All research confirms that the parents' contribution to the problem cannot be understated, especially if they ridicule their children, make unfavorable comparisons between siblings, and treat the siblings differently.

Generally, the suppression of feelings, the absence of a balancing ***mental power of compensation****** for achievement, and the constant attempt by the sufferer to hide the problem by pretense could lead to mental illness and neurotic behavior. The afflicted person's self-consciousness and his or her attempts to conceal the symptoms by constantly projecting a false image could cause anxiety and psychological pain, and persistent anxiety often leads to depression. Chronic suffering from anxiety is usually caused by mental isolation and constant pretension. This results in a loss of words when communicating, difficulty in making friends, and a feeling of loneliness. Because of overcompensation, the sufferers are often perceived as being snobbish instead of shy, which adds to their isolation and rejection.

*** **Mental power of compensation** is a tendency to make up for underdevelopment of physical or mental functioning through interest and training, usually within a relatively normal range of development. The power of compensation is based on the principle of everybody has some skills others don't have that can be triggered to enhance these special skills to achieve excellence. Special skills could be triggered when the mental power of compensation is present and capabilities are stimulated and helped to develop by motivation.

It's possible to overcome an inferiority complex through the following methods:

- Avoid the type of people who tend to compare themselves favorably to you with the intention to bolster their own image or strengthen their position at your expense. Lack of awareness in your social and work environments can make you a target or a prey for such individuals.

- Avoid people who criticize others unconstructively or without the facts or the intellectual capacity to back up their criticism. These people either wish to inflate their own egos at others' expense or are afflicted with an inferiority complex. Look deeper to discover their motives. Do not allow them to inflict you with self-doubt. Learn to ignore unsubstantiated negative comments made against you.

- Have an open mind for accepting constructive criticism.

- Strengthen your beliefs with knowledge, and strive to move positively in a forward and more successful direction. Adopt the notion that everyone is entitled to his or her own opinion, including you.

- Develop self-confidence and self-awareness to become more independent and capable of determining your own self-worth.

- Understand flaws realistically: any flaw you may have is not as bad as you think it is; having flaws is not the same as not having many positive qualities. Everybody has some flaws, as nobody is perfect.

- Love yourself in a healthy way; be determined, have an open mind for positive ideas, and develop inner strength to counter the negatives; be a healthy narcissist.

- Be humble by remembering that there are some who have achieved more than you have and others who have achieved less, which places you somewhere in the middle. A middle position is a modest one that can be used as a springboard for your motivation to do better.

- Finally, to overcome the problem of feeling inferior, consider the principle of "everybody has some skills that others don't have." This can be used as a trigger to enhance your special skills to achieve excellence. Special skills can only be triggered when the positive mental power of compensation is present and capabilities are stimulated and helped to develop by motivation.

Body Image

The commercial world, the media, and the press are constantly bombarding the public, including children, with distorted information about body image; even near-perfect children find faults with themselves, and this affects their self-esteem. This feeling, if not countered, could become entrenched and persist throughout adulthood. Body image is a by-product of one's personal opinion and social and cultural influences. The personal opinion usually relates to the individual's perception of his or her physical appearance, which can be completely different from others' perception of that individual's look. The social and cultural influences relate to family trends, schools, religion, gender, peers, ethnicity, socioeconomic status, biological predisposition, celebrities, fashion and cosmetics, product promotion, and so on. The individual's perception regarding his or her body—fat or skinny, tall or short, beautiful or ugly, and so on—can cause anxiety, and when anxiety persists, a personality disorder often follows.

Research shows that the importance attached to physical appearance decreases with age. Although physical appearance is still important for mature people, body image takes on a different meaning as the functional aspects of the body begin to take precedence. One thing to remember is that as the body changes, so does the image of oneself. Researchers tell you: if you focus only on the negatives of your look, you will lower your self-esteem. Self-esteem is as stated earlier: it is about how much you value yourself and how much you feel other people value you. It is also about accepting yourself as you really are, and this acceptance can affect your mental stability and your behavior.

Understandably, consciousness of your body image intensifies at the onset of puberty, when your body goes through many changes. These changes include mental changes, such as the desire to be accepted by friends and relatives and to be compared favorably to others. At this time of changes, you should remember that not everyone grows or develops the same way. If at any stage of your life you want to change your appearance, choose only what is realistically possible. The early teen years are a time when you become more aware of celebrities and media images and how you fit in. This is the time when you should remember that celebrities and images are too ideal and artificial. Think of the hours they spend on their images with the help of so many professionals in the field of presentation and promotion. If you mentally strip these celebrities of their cosmetics, Botox, facelifts, surgeries, and expensive gear, you'll see that not only are their images unreal, but their personalities are synthetic, too. Above all, many of these synthetic personalities are afflicted with personality disorders. Accordingly, you can conclude that you are much better than most of them, provided that you have developed a pleasant personality and confidence. And above all, you should remember that you're real, and they're not.

A positive body image most likely will make you accept yourself the way you really are, even if you don't fit the image that is presented by the media. This healthy attitude allows you to explore other aspects of growing up, such as friendship, self-awareness, and independence. A positive and optimistic attitude, combined with a healthy lifestyle, is an essential element of happiness and the building of self-esteem. After all, it is your body, and you have to learn to live with it and care for it through physical fitness and proper personal hygiene. And remember that self-belief and confidence are the most important elements of beauty. You should never forget that there is probably no one in the world who doesn't see something he or she doesn't like about himself or herself, whether physical or psychological. And remember that there will always be many others ahead of you and many behind you, both physically and mentally.

Finally, if your body image and low self-esteem are affecting your well-being and you feel powerless to control your negative emotions, you should seek counseling.

CHAPTER 6

Mental Health Problems

Mental health problems relate to distorted thoughts or feelings and abnormal or unstable behavior. Unstable or abnormal behavior is thought to afflict about 15 percent of the population of Western countries. Psychiatrists have developed systems for classifying unstable behavior into two groups: personality disorders (some of which are discussed in chapter 5) and psychoses. Another common group of disorders is called anxiety disorders.

Mental health problems can be difficult to recognize, especially when access to professional help is limited and in many instances unaffordable or stigmatic. It is more so when part of the solution is the ability to identify youth who are at risk of developing problems, while no efforts are made and no funding is allocated to the task. Western governments are well aware that such a complex problem requires a complex solution but often turn a blind eye due to lack of funding. The shortsightedness of these governments is reflected in their ignorance of the fact that treating people in the early stages of these problems—a mildly compulsive personality disorder, for example—costs a lot less than treating patients with entrenched psychoses or antisocial behaviors. Research shows that the longer a person is psychosis-free, the easier his or her condition is to treat at the onset of the symptoms.

Another aspect of mental health is psychosis that is caused by exposure to violence through wars. For example, the wars in other countries that are initiated by the United States' expansionist policy to meet its need of energy and other resources are causing traumatic experiences. Soldiers become traumatized by the killings, especially when their victims are women and children. Many traumatized soldiers end up with mental problems, and many commit suicide. On January 20, 2013, former Secretary of Defense Leon Panetta stated that military suicide is now an epidemic. He also said that the last decade of fighting two wars holds "lots of lessons" to be learned about the human side of this prolonged warfare and how we get a handle on problems such as traumatic brain injury and post-traumatic stress disorder. Military and medical leaders have been searching for answers for the suicide epidemic ever since the numbers began increasing among soldiers and marines in 2005. Researchers see it as directly linked to the effects of combat and frequent deployments. The time psychological conflicts surface is after soldiers return home.

The same problem afflicts British soldiers, the US allies. According to the BBC's *Panorama*, in 2012, suicides by former British military personnel exceeded the number of those who died in action in Afghanistan during the same period.

The Impact of Bullying and Cyberbullying

Bullying

Bullying is the social degradation of a victim by an individual or a group either for the purpose of increasing its own self-comfort or for enjoyment. It can be emotional, verbal, or physical and driven by racial, religious, gender, or sexual considerations. According to the US National Center for Education (in the 2008-2009 School Crime Supplement), bullying can be classified as direct or indirect, and it is a social aggression. It has been observed that males are more likely to be physically aggressive, while females tend to bully by exclusion and mockery. However, the video recording feature on mobile devices and instant posting on the Internet is encouraging some females to become physically aggressive as well.

Bullying is estimated to affect one in four school kids. Without corrective measures, bullying usually extends beyond children in the school yard and into the adult workplace. In either case, it affects productivity and ultimately the country's economy. Bullying can also have serious effects on the targeted person's physical and mental health.

Research shows that a bully is usually a person who does not value himself or herself, feels inferior, or has been a victim of violence. Bullying for such a person becomes an avenue for feeling more powerful. Often bullying becomes the individual's way of dealing with his or her own psychological problems. A bully may also be motivated by jealousy, ignorance, resentment, and fear; he or she may act out in order to conceal shame and anxiety or to maintain a false image.

Bullying in all its forms has devastating effects on children's development, self-esteem, emotions, motivation to study, and family relations. The tragedy of bullying is that the bully ends up becoming antisocial and the bullied end up with anxiety disorders. Furthermore, one of the consequences is the eventual character assassination of others. And ultimately this could turn into gun violence. (For gun violence, see chapter 7.)

Some children are victims, and others are bullies or onlookers. The onlookers are not only the ones who directly observe the bullying, but also those who know about it. They play a major role in reinforcing the behavior by watching and doing nothing. The onlookers must remember that bullying can happen to them and that they can make a positive contribution by reporting the bullying or helping a bullied friend. If the bully in the group is not challenged early, he or she will assume that bullying is accepted and embraced by the group. A bully who encounters no negative response from onlookers is encouraged to continue—and even escalate—the behavior. Unless the onlookers take remedial action, the culture of bullying can become a major social and economic problem for the country and cause psychological damage to both the bully and the bullied.

There is a growing body of research that indicates that individuals, whether children or adults, who are persistently subjected to abusive behavior are at risk for stress-related illness, which can sometimes lead to suicide. Those who have been the targets of bullying can suffer from long-term emotional and behavioral problems.

Adding to these problems are the modern communication technologies, which are becoming the source of more violence, bullying, and intimidation, especially among the younger generation. Modern technologies such as the Internet and mobile phones have introduced a new form of bullying: cyberbullying. This has increased the incidence of bullying to a dangerous level. (For more on cyberbullying, see below.)

In his book, *Bullying at Schools: How Successful Can Intervention Be?* (2004), Peter K. Smith confirms some key points about bullying:

- Certain children are more at risk than others.
- The children are both the victims and the bullies.
- The most tragic outcome of bullying is the victim's suicide.
- The introduction of early intervention programs by schools to prevent bullying is effective. The program should be supplemented with appropriate supervision and monitoring outside the classroom.
- The most important elements of such a program are recognizing the problem, developing strategies to counter bullying, and coordinating actions. The

program should also include guidelines on how to discourage bullying and how to help victims.

- To counter bullying, relevant techniques should be taught. These include assertiveness, anger management, and bystanders' helpful behavior.

It should be acknowledged that bullying and intimidation are widespread problems. They occur not only within schools but within religious groups and families and even internationally. Becoming aware of these problems and learning how to deal with them is essential for maintaining one's sanity. It's of paramount importance to eradicate all forms of bullying and intimidation by doing the following:

- First, as discussed in chapter 2, is by having highly qualified and well-trained teachers who can deal with psychological problems.
- Second is forming special-education classes for problem youths.
- Third is involving the families of the young people who are developing problems.
- Fourth is the need for adequate funding to enable schools to deal with the problem. This includes continuous updating of information for teachers and adequate funding for mental health intervention—with less emphasis on prescribing medication.
- Fifth is destigmatizing mental health problems to encourage people to seek timely help.

- Last is recognizing that all actions listed above will have little effect without a reduction in the media's sensationalizing of crimes and the glorification of horror and violent movies and video games. (For more on the impact of violent movies and video games, see chapter 7.)

Cyberbullying

Cyberbullying is a modern form of bullying that is difficult for parents to detect because the bullies can hide their identities. Cyberbullying can take place through e-mail, instant messaging, text messaging, websites, social networking sites, and so on. It's defined as using information and communication technologies to support deliberate, repeated, and hostile behavior by an individual or a group that is intended to harm another person or other people. The National Crime Prevention Council considers it a crime when the Internet, cell phones, or other devices are used to send or post text or images intended to hurt or embarrass another person. A cyberbully may be a person whom the target knows or a stranger; the bully may be anonymous and may solicit involvement of other people online who do not even know the target.

As for adults' cyberbullying, it has criminal consequences just as physical bullying does. The distinction between children's and adults' cyberbullying is that adults' cyberbullying abuse can be classified as cyberstalking or cyberharassment. It is an extension of physical stalking. Understanding why it is happening can help determine the action to be taken to remedy the problem. A repeated pattern of actions and harassment against an intended target constitutes cyberstalking. Cyberstalking frequently takes place in public forums or on social media or online information sites and is intended to threaten a victim's earnings, employment, reputation, or safety. Many cyberstalkers try to damage the reputation of their victim and encourage others to do the same. Cyberstalking may include making false accusations, monitoring, making threats, gathering information in order to harass, and causing damage to data or equipment. It also includes identity theft and solicitation of minors for sex. While it could be limited to posting rumors about a person on the Internet with the intention of provoking hatred or denigration of the intended target, it may go further, including publishing defamatory and humiliating materials about the victim. It could include the disclosure of the victim's personal information or threats to publish personal information and rumors.

As for the teen cyberbullies, The National Crime Prevention Association lists tactics often used by this group. They may do any of the following:

- pretend they are other people online to trick others
- spread lies and rumors about victims
- trick people into revealing personal information
- send or forward mean text messages
- post pictures of victims without their consent

The consequences of cyberbullying have a devastating psychological impact on victims. According to the *Journal of Psychosocial Research on Cyberspace*, based on respondents' feedback, victims of cyberbullying suffer from low self-esteem, loneliness, disillusionment, and distrust of people. The more extreme impacts were self-harm and, in some cases, suicide.

In Western countries there are laws aimed at the protection of children from online harassment and from predators, as well as laws to protect adult victims of cyberstalking and harassment. The Global Cyber Law Database (GCLD) is in the process of becoming a comprehensive source of cyber laws for all countries. Cyberstalking laws are designed to prosecute people for using electronic means to repeatedly harass or threaten someone online. There are resources dedicated to helping adult victims deal with cyberbullies legally and effectively. Two of the steps recommended are to record everything and contact police.

There is now a great deal of hard evidence regarding the physical and mental harm that continued bullying does to vulnerable children. The statistics prove that children who continually engage in bullying are more likely than others to engage in criminal activities. With the involvement of all concerned—the government, schools, and parents—the cycle can be broken for both the victims and the perpetrators. Antibullying programs should be developed by engaging police, students, teachers, and parents to help break the cycle. Such programs must instill, reinforce, and reward the values of empathy, compassion, and acceptance.

The Impact of Drug and Alcohol Abuse

Teaching social skills early can prevent future crises related to drug and alcohol abuse, criminal and violent behavior, and mental illness. It's the idea of using the prevention-better-than-the-cure approach rather than taking action when it's too late. New research has revealed that young people are at risk of developing neurotic depression, schizophrenia, and other psychotic disorders when they are addicted to an illicit drug. The research also found that heavy users of cannabis, cocaine, and amphetamines experienced their first symptoms at a younger age than those who abstained or took only one drug. Drugs are known to increase the risk of early development of psychotic illnesses. If the age of onset can be delayed, the illness in a person who is predisposed to schizophrenia can potentially be helped by early intervention. Early use of drugs is a risk for all young people, not just those predisposed to schizophrenia, because the brain is still developing until the early twenties. Drugs can derail normal development by altering the plasticity of the brain as well as the wiring and connections and can have many other long-standing physical effects.

The majority of young people become addicted to drugs and alcohol initially by experimenting in a social scene, often due to peer pressure. Others use the substances as a way to cope with the stress of school or work or, in some cases, family tension or marital distress. Gradually, drugs and alcohol become the substitute for personal satisfaction and self-fulfillment or are used to compensate for feelings of guilt and inadequacy. When drugs and alcohol are easily accessible, socially acceptable, and useful for temporarily escaping life's problems or manufacturing self-fulfillment, addiction becomes most likely.

The use and misuse of alcohol and other drugs is one of the more controversial issues in our society and often a source of conflict between generations and sections of society. Alcohol and other drugs are powerful substances with the potential to harm users or to tempt them into addiction. It is important to take care of one's health by not poisoning his or her body. Although alcohol and drug use is becoming an accepted part of some of the youth social scenes today, the danger is lurking for tomorrow. Drugs and alcohol can alter one's behavior and psyche, and this, in turn, can damage one's personality and social standing. Drug abuse may sound acceptable and normal today, but one must think about what it can do to his or her future. Before an individual becomes part of such a social scene, he or she must consider the fact that one can become impulsive, dependent, and controlled by drugs and alcohol. Furthermore, if at a later date when this individual's well-being is under threat and he or she decides to quit (if it's not too late), he or she will need considerable professional support.

A trusted friend, who has been there and done that, will most likely tell you: "Consider the fact that drugs and alcohol can lower your resistance to self-harm and can hurt your other friends and family, besides destroying your own immune system. This is in addition to the financial ruin, trouble with the law, diminished sex life, and other social consequences it can lead to. Above all, drugs and alcohol can lead to loss of reality, misery, decreased confidence, and many psychological problems, such as heightened anxiety, depression, and even psychosis."

To take control of your destiny, the trusted friend will also say that you should consider the following:

- First, observe or talk to some others who have been there and done that and now deeply regret what they've done.

- Second, focus on the long-term disadvantages instead of the temporary highs.

- Third, consider reducing your intake to gradually change your routine and reduce the need for admission to a specialized institution. Behavioral interventions and medications have helped many people reduce or discontinue drug and alcohol abuse, but the cold-turkey approach is the better option, provided you have the willpower to get you through.

- Fourth, talk to a person or people you trust about your problem and your desire to quit.

- Finally, remember that dependency is a disease. According to US statistics, drugs and alcohol contribute to over 50 percent of all suicides and to over 50 percent of all violent crimes. They are also responsible for over 60 percent of admissions to hospital emergency departments and are the cause of over 50 percent of all traffic accidents, with many of these being fatal.

Ultimately, if you've decided to destroy your life, drugs and alcohol are the answer.

Schizophrenia

Schizophrenia is a common form of chronic psychotic disorder related to the impairment of a person's mental capacity to recognize reality, communicate, and deal with life's demands. It's a functional disorder, also called a mood disorder. The major symptoms, aside from paranoia, delusions, and hallucinations, are disorganized speech and behavior, lack of emotional expression, and apathy. It usually starts with a distortion of perception: for example, sounds may seem louder than usual to the individual, or he or she may develop unfounded beliefs. As the disorder progresses, the afflicted person may feel that he or she is being watched, hear sounds or voices that don't exist, or imagine that he or she is being touched. The individual will feel frightened often. Some sufferers may believe that the voices they hear are those of God or the devil.

Note: The following discussion deals with schizophrenia as it relates to addiction to drugs and alcohol only. It's not meant to deal with the wider aspects of schizophrenia.

Individuals who have drug- and alcohol-induced schizophrenic psychosis tend to have a greater awareness of their psychosis and tend to have higher levels of depression and suicidal thinking compared to individuals who have a primary psychotic illness. Although some sufferers with a mild form of the disorder can be cured, others with severe symptoms—especially those who suffered for a long duration without treatment—are not fully curable. Therefore, the sooner one attempts to rid himself or herself of addiction, the better his or her chances of recovery. The best preventative measure, however, is to avoid all drugs and alcohol that have been associated with the development of schizophrenia.

It should be noted that schizophrenia is often accompanied by other conditions, such as anxiety and depression. Also to be noted is that evidence shows a direct link between earlier onset of psychotic illness and cannabis use. About half of those with schizophrenia use drugs or alcohol excessively. The more often cannabis is used; the more likely a person is to develop a psychotic illness, with frequent use being correlated with twice the risk of psychosis and schizophrenia.

Schizophrenia can be genetic, environmental, or induced. Induced schizophrenia relates to the use of medicine, alcohol, or illegal drugs. Research shows that addiction to alcohol and various psychoactive substances, especially the illegal ones, are causing or exacerbating psychotic states of the addicted. When an individual becomes a compulsive and repetitive user, he or she is classified as substance dependent. The medical approach to physiological dependence requires the gradual development of tolerance, leading to withdrawal symptoms when use is reduced or stopped. Both abuse and dependence are distinct from addiction, which involves a compulsion to continue using the substance despite the negative consequences. Furthermore, illegally produced drugs may have contaminants. Withdrawal from the drugs or their contaminants can cause additional health issues, not to mention social issues (e.g., the individual becomes vulnerable to both criminal abuse and legal punishment).

According to a study by Dr. Rebecca McKetin (2013), users of methamphetamine are five times likelier to suffer psychotic symptoms while taking the drug than those with a preexisting psychotic condition. The study was published in *JAMA Psychiatry*. McKetin said, "There have always been questions about causality from those who say methamphetamine users aren't turned mad by the drug but have a preexisting psychotic condition. What's unique about this study is that it excludes those users (with a preexisting psychotic condition) and still finds such a strong link between use and psychotic symptoms in a large cohort over a period of years."

Treatment for psychotic symptoms usually consists of medication to suppress the dopamine receptor activity or psychotherapy or both; severe cases may require permanent hospitalization. The affected person may have difficulty thinking rationally or concentrating over a long period of time. He or she is likely to show disturbed speech, may hear voices, and may have persistent unfounded beliefs, such as believing he or she is being persecuted or controlled. These symptoms can cause problems in managing work, studies, or relationships, and can lead to social isolation or hostility from others.

CHAPTER 7

Gun Violence

Gun Violence in the United States

The US screen culture of violence spills over into real life and often leads to copycat action that causes the death of many innocent Americans. Culture is not about killing people with assault rifles. Culture is meant to be something positive about a society, but instead society is afflicted with the massacre of innocent people. Culture is comprised of the mental and spiritual aspects of a nation. It develops through an evolutionary social process that coincides with the sophistication of a people relative to their scientific and economic progress. Social and environmental conditions of a nation are behind the emergence and development of culture, which in turn determines the system of interaction among people. Unfortunately, the United States' culture of violence is reflected not only from within, but also in its aggression toward other countries.

Currently, there are over three hundred million weapons in the hands of Americans—as many as the US population. It gets worse: when politicians just mention the need for gun control, the sale of weapons increases dramatically—especially rapid-fire, semiautomatic guns and ammunition. Even worse, 40 percent of guns sold require no background check, and thirty Americans are murdered every day. In some states, a teenager can purchase an AK-47 semiautomatic assault rifle at a gun show without having to show ID or submit to a background check.

Because of the power of the National Rifle Association, no president is able to stop the violence in the United States. This is despite the fact that more Americans died by these guns than all the Americans who died in all US wars, including the American Civil War. As a matter of fact, according to statistics presented on January 18, 2013 by Mark Shields of Public Broadcasting Service (PBS), "42 years after Robert Kennedy was shot dead, 1,260,703 Americans died in firearms—by firearms. In the total history of the United States in every war, in the Revolutionary War, and all the world's wars, 659,000 Americans have died in combat, twice as many in one-fifth the time."

Worst yet, there is nothing that will stop international terrorists when they become more powerful or desperate from gradually settling in the United States, proceeding with their agenda, and using military assault rifles on Americans. It is ironic: if terrorists kill Americans, all hell breaks loose to find the culprits so that they can be tortured and punished. Yet when an American kills other Americans en masse, no politician is prepared to stand up to the extremist gun lobby groups that are hiding behind the **Second Amendment to the Constitution**, * which gives Americans the right to bear arms. Despite repeated tragedies and talk about how to stop mass murders, the extremist **National**

Rifle Association (NRA) **—supported by **Jews for the Preservation of Firearms Ownership (JPFO)** *** and arms manufacturers—is able to prevent politicians from making any move on gun control. The power of these groups has achieved the entrenchment of ownership of assault weapons in US culture.

Unfortunately, the violence in US culture is spreading to other countries that are exposed to the popular US entertainment industry through violent movies and videos games. The younger generation of other countries cannot escape the onslaught of their negative influence.

* The Second Amendment to the Constitution is contained in the Bill of Rights and protects the right of people to keep and bear arms. It refers to the concept that people have an individual right to own and carry weapons. It was adopted on December 15, 1791, along with the rest of the Bill of Rights. It is about self-defense. Americans generally argue about the meaning of self-defense and common defense. (US farmers want to have both.)

** The National Rifle Association (NRA): The NRA is a US nonprofit lobbying group that advocates for the protection of the Second Amendment and the promotion of firearm ownership rights, as well as marksmanship, firearm safety, and the protection of hunting and self-defense in the United States. The NRA sponsors firearm-safety training courses, as well as marksmanship events featuring shooting skill and sports. As of the 1999 survey, it was considered by lawmakers and congressional staffers that the NRA is the most influential lobbying group. Its political activity is based on the principle that gun ownership is a civil liberty protected by the Second Amendment of the Bill of Rights, and the NRA refers to itself as

the oldest continuously operating civil rights organization in the United States. It was founded in 1871. According to its website, the NRA has over four million members. The Institute for Legislative Action (ILA) is the lobbying arm of the National Rifle Association of America. Eight US presidents have been NRA members.

*** Jews for the Preservation of Firearms Ownership (JPFO): *The group was founded in 1989 by a former firearms dealer, Mr. Aaron Zelman (1946–2010). It's a nonprofit and tax-exempt educational and civil rights organization—or so it claims. It's a group dedicated to the preservation of gun rights in the United States and to encouraging Americans to understand and defend all of the Bill of Rights for everyone. The JPFO interprets the Second Amendment as recognizing a preexisting natural right of individuals to keep and bear arms. It equates gun control with totalitarianism and attempts to prove that genocide is linked to gun control.*

Aaron Zelman—the founder of group—was famous for saying, "Anyone who is lawfully adjudicated unfit to carry a firearm should not be on the street in the first place; he should be in prison or in a mental institution. We've thrown the baby (our personal liberties) out with the bathwater, making us helpless to protect ourselves from armed criminals and lunatics. And who promotes this delusional illogic the most fervently?—politicians and the law enforcement hierarchy."

He also pointed out that every holocaust, starting with the Armenian and up to the Rwandan, occurred after the population targeted for extinction was disarmed. He was appalled that so many Jewish politicians and influential Jewish public officials and spokespeople actually advocate citizen disarmament. He believed that Jews should be the last people on earth to support gun control.

The irony is that Jews, especially the Israelis—supported by the religious nationalist Zionists and US extremists—are now armed to the teeth and ruthlessly killing many unarmed and innocent people with gunships, tanks, drones, and assault rifles in the process of colonizing Palestine. All this is when the Jewish moral and religious mandate is for righteous self-defense and the defense of the innocent. Unfortunately, in Palestine the Jews are replicating what the Nazis did to Jews in Germany.

As noted by L. D. Lewis, a journalist and author who has been covering the Israeli/Palestinian conflict for six years and who came up against the sheer racism and coordinated efforts of Zionist propaganda, "The apartheid system that Israel embraces, the euphemisms and omissions clandestinely hidden in its claims of democracy, hide nothing else but sheer racism." He exposes the ugly side of Zionism and Israel, the racism and disregard for non-Jewish human life. He's written extensively on this issue and is often labeled anti-Semitic for his honest presentation. (For more on extreme Zionism, see my book *Israel vs. America vs. the World.*)

As for the Second Amendment, the time lapse since it was originally adopted should be taken into consideration. It was adopted in the eighteenth century when the majority of Americans were farmers or farm workers, as farming was the dominant occupation and people's living reality was totally different from the present reality. It is ironic that at the time when the amendment to the Constitution was adopted, the military-style assault rifles didn't exist; this renders the current constitutional debate irrelevant. The sad part of the story is that the death toll within the United States from guns is far higher than the loss of US soldiers fighting for the US empire around the world.

The problem with the current debate is that different vested interests present different interpretations of the amendment to suit their own agendas, interpretations that, in many cases, are far from the amendment's original intent. Furthermore, the current debate doesn't include the evolution of language from the time the amendment was written, as well as the nature of the language generally where every word has many different meanings. Languages are notorious for creating conflict and fragmentation. This can be illustrated by examining any law or constitution of any country that ends up at the center of endless arguments, many of which lead to referral to the Supreme Court for interpretation. Often the interpretation and the final judgment are not unanimous but are decided by a majority of one. To further illustrate the problem with the language, just look at how religious and political leaders use the language. These leaders manipulate, distort, and exploit the language in their application of mass psychology to achieve their objectives. They use catchy phrases and lies, omit facts, and develop semantic disagreements to create subjective groups and sects. In the process, they fragment the society. A sense of timing assisted by intellect, speaking skills, and charisma are the main characteristics of one skilled in manipulation and exploitation of the masses. Generally, the ability to manipulate and exploit the masses relates directly to the emotional and social intelligences of the sinister leader and the ignorance or the apathy of the majority.

Amending any constitution and amending an amendment to an amendment should not be a major problem for a mature nation. A sophisticated nation with fundamental wisdom should be capable of updating its constitution to suit today's conditions. This can be achieved by compromise and moderation and by looking at the underlying values of the original document and applying these values to the current realities. Pressure applied to politicians by a vocal extreme Right minority is a recipe for conflict. As always, eventually one extreme provokes and creates an opposite extreme, especially when the first extreme is dogmatic and ideological.

The question should be asked, if the Second Amendment to the Constitution is causing so many deaths and so much destruction to the US social fabric, what is the purpose of having it or not amending it? Generally, constitutions are written to coincide with the prevailing social environment and the realities of the time and are constantly reviewed and amended to suit changing realities. They're not meant to be treated as gospel, though even the Bible was amended, sanitized, and canonized almost four hundred years after Christ. And since it was amended, many translations and interpretations have been added to it, including the Ten Commandments. Furthermore, many ridiculous aspects of the Bible are skillfully glossed over by religious leaders. Constitutions, likewise, should not be treated so dogmatically.

During the United States' prosperous times in the early 1990s, and until recently, gun violence was decreasing. Contributing to this drop in violence were higher rates of incarceration and shifts in police practices, including targeting certain neighborhoods (as opposed to the earlier approach of just randomly patrolling the streets). What also contributed to the improvements in certain cities were upgraded social programs and better public housing, especially where high-density public housing had been disbursed to some degree. Unfortunately, however, with the current economic decline, the United States' gun violence is on the rise again. This is mainly due to the impact of extreme capitalism, high unemployment, and the lack of fair distribution of wealth. The United States is now dealing with the by-products of generational poverty, socioeconomic disparities and deprivation, with no solution in sight. (For the impact of extreme capitalism, please refer back to chapter 3 of this book and chapter 4 of *Israel vs. America vs. the World.*)

As for the National Rifle Association and its lobbying power, it has aggravated the problem for the United States, and now its leadership wants to solve the problem with more guns. In December 2012, following the massacre of twenty-eight people (twenty of whom were children) at Sandy Hook Elementary School in Newtown, Connecticut, President Barack Obama advocated the instituting of gun control. To quell violence in the United States, the president commissioned a new White House task force to counter the nation's strong culture of gun ownership. In response, and a week after the massacre, the NRA's executive vice president, Wayne LaPierre, urged lawmakers to station armed police officers in all schools by the time students returned from the Christmas break in January 2013. His argument was, "The only thing that stops a bad guy with a gun is a good guy with a gun." He has emphatically ruled out supporting greater controls on weapons or ammunition in the United States. He said, "If it's crazy to call for putting police and armed security in our schools, then call me crazy." You can be the judge. He called Obama's planned legislation phony and claimed it was built on lies that have been found out. He doesn't consider guns the problem; instead, he believes the problem is the criminal, which is a policing problem. This is his solution, instead of trying to stop the bad guys from getting guns in the first place.

Unfortunately, the NRA's argument regarding the good guy with a gun versus the bad guy with a gun lacks logic. It ignores the fact that before a criminal or a mentally deranged person reaches his or her intended target, the first target will be the good guy with a gun, which will result in more good guys getting killed. The NRA's drive to fill all US schools with more deadly guns and ammunition is revolting and irresponsible. Allowing people to legally purchase and use military-style assault rifles with high-capacity ammunition clips designed for mass killings is extremism with no sense of guilt. Worse yet, there is no national database of mentally ill people to prevent them from being excluded from owning assault rifles. Even if there were a database of the mentally ill, it would not stop the carnage. Consider the following:

- First, fewer mentally ill people will seek psychiatric help in order to avoid being entered into the database.
- Second, assault weapons can be purchased in many different ways, such as by private sales, on the black market, on the Internet, or from other states that have no restrictions on the sale of weapons.
- Third, nothing can stop people with bad intentions.
- Fourth, it is extremely difficult to identify individuals who need help.
- Fifth, a Republican-controlled Congress is a major stumbling block against gun control legislation.

Worse yet, as a reaction to the Newtown massacre, many US states are in the process of allowing schoolteachers to carry weapons, and now teachers are flocking to training sessions. While teachers train themselves, progun politicians are crafting legislation to make sure teachers can legally do so. This is the way extremist Americans solve negative problems—with negative solutions. And the country ends up with a lose-lose outcome. Above all, there will always be different laws in different states that are in conflict with federal laws. Here it is worth pointing out that some extreme

NRA members believe in the right to take up arms to resist government policies they consider oppressive, even when these policies have been adopted by elected officials and subjected to review by an independent judiciary.

According to the NRA, most of the proposals that have to do with firearms are simply feel-good proposals that have been tried in the past and won't work or won't have any real impact. The outgoing NRA president, David Keene, said, "The group might support universal background checks, if they could be made to work." He further said, "The difficulty comes in when you're talking about you and me as next-door neighbors and you buy a new shotgun and want to sell one to me. How do you enforce a background check on that?"

Psychologists are fully aware that one of the main obstacles to preventing violence is identifying individuals who most need psychological help. This obstacle is acknowledged as extremely hard to overcome. Therefore, until a total ban on gun ownership is implemented, mental health problems will always cause conflict with violent crimes and school safety. With Congress controlled by the Republicans, who are in turn controlled by the extremist Tea Party, the chance of their approving any form of gun control is remote. The call for stricter prohibition against military assault-style weapons is not only rejected by the Republicans, but also by some Democrats, not to mention the gun lobby. The debate in the Senate is narrowed to background checks, which will have little impact on gun violence in the United States. The Senate's plan wouldn't require background checks for private sales between individuals. The number of guns in circulation would increase further in the panicked buying to beat the new laws. Besides, criminals, to avoid background checks, are not going to buy assault weapons legally. Background checks will not prevent the next shooting or violent crime, and they will not keep schoolchildren safe. Gun violence can only be controlled by a total firearm ban, zero-tolerance laws, proper education (including funding, especially for poor and disadvantaged schools), and youth violence prevention and intervention programs. Here it should not be forgotten that many suicides are directly related to the accessibility of guns.

Following all the noises and the president's campaign for background checks, in April 2013, the Senate voted down the proposed legislation. An angry Barack Obama decried a "shameful day for Washington" after the Senate blocked a bipartisan plan for extended background checks for gun buyers. Despite emotional pleas from the families of victims of the Newtown shootings and broad public support nationwide, the plan to extend background checks to online and gun-show sales failed to clear the Senate, as 90 percent of Republicans voted against the idea. The idea was to close the loophole that lets dangerous criminals buy a gun without a background check. Mr. Obama accused the gun lobby of spreading lies about what the reform was meant to do. The Senate also knocked back a proposal to ban automatic weapons and high-capacity magazines of the type used in the Sandy Hook massacre.

Mr. Obama also said that the spreading of untruths by the gun lobby about the legislation served a purpose because those lies upset an intense minority of gun owners, and that in turn intimidated a lot of senators. The legislative failure occurred despite public opinion polls showing that as many as 90 percent of Americans supported the proposal. All this wasn't enough to beat the power of the gun lobby, led by the National Rifle Association, which spread fear about the establishment of a national gun database. The NRA and its allies claimed that the bill would create a Big Brother-style gun registry, when the bill intended to do the opposite.

As can be seen, the NRA controls the debate and is capable of derailing any logical approach to save lives. One of these approaches is to allocate psychologists to schools, who, with the help of the teachers, can identify students in need of mental health treatment and establish a database of individuals with mental illnesses. The main point here is to start somewhere in trying to determine in advance who might be capable of violence. As a starting point in the prevention of gun violence, the United States is in desperate need of prevention programs, including the establishment of a database starting from the early years of school.

According to Dr. Paramjit Joshi of the Children's National Medical Center, "The issue is that young children and adolescents sometimes will have aggressive behaviors early on. And I think the whole issue of trying to access care early on would go a long way in trying to prevent some of the more aggressive and violent behaviors as these youngsters get older. So I really applaud President Obama's recommendations and proposals that he's put forth about early intervention, early identification, and increasing the number of resources, both in schools and also generally in the mental health system." He expressed the thought that the most important thing is to provide the services in the school systems by having counselors, psychologists, and mental health social workers in the school setting, because that's where children spend most of their day. It's easily accessible. And, in fact, a mental health in school act was proposed in **The 112th Congress****** that put forth funding for this particular intervention.

**** **The 112th Congress** was the meeting of the legislative branch of the United States federal government, from January 3, 2011, until January 3, 2013. It convened in Washington, DC, on January 3, 2011, and ended on January 3, 2013, seventeen days before the end of the presidential term to which Barack Obama was elected in 2008. Senators elected to regular terms in 2006 completed those terms in this Congress. This Congress included the last House of Representatives elected from congressional districts that were apportioned based on the 2000 census.

The proposal is an indirect solution to the problem, which can improve general mental health functioning among children, teenagers, and adults. Allocating more resources into understanding violence can lead to understanding the causes of that violence and the development of prevention methods and treatments. Therefore, allocation of extra resources for early intervention can go a long way toward arriving at a solution.

Opponents of the proposal might say that there are potential ramifications and express concern that it will inhibit people from getting mental health treatment if they feel like going and talking to their doctor about themselves. It could likewise deter people from seeking treatment for their depression because they don't want to be hospitalized as potentially homicidal. It is true it may deter people from coming forward to talk about their feelings. But there's a fine line between keeping the public safe and protecting their privacy. With children and teenagers, parental consent is always sought. In this case, privacy is not a major issue when dealing with children and teenagers, compared to dealing with adults. Early identification, prevention, and treatment before teenagers get to the point of dangerous aggression are necessary for the protection of society.

Unfortunately, however, judging by the high rate of suicide among teenagers and war veterans, there is gross neglect due to lack of resources and funding. There is no point in identifying more patients when there are insufficient resources to deal with more patients. It is a classic case of politicians talking about a major problem to show they care, but when it comes to funding the solution, the money is not there. It's funny that the majority of politicians throughout the Western world behave in the same way.

The Impact of Violent Movies and Video Games

Many researchers point to the negative influence the entertainment industry has on people's psyche and behavior. The assertion that violent movies and video games cause kids to become violent has existed for a long time. Some researchers have noted that, generally, violent movies and video games are leading to violent behavior among children and adults. More specifically, there has been extensive research on the impact of violent movies and video games on kids' behavior, especially kids aged eleven or twelve—being the most impressionable and impulsive age during the period of transition from a child into a teenager. Some research points to a direct link, while other studies point to the problem as addiction to the games, which causes the kids to become isolated. Early exposure to violence can eventually turn some children into violent adults.

Sadly, the marketing of violent movies and video games aimed at children is not regulated. According to Jim Steyer, the founder and CEO of Common Sense Media, which focuses on media consumption by children, "Regulation is not censorship; it is sanity." Steyer is adamant that violent movies and video games must not be marketed to children at the age of eleven or twelve.

Whether regulation is censorship or sanity, without gun control, no positive outcome should be expected. Teenagers' and adults' violence is aggravated by the free access to guns and assault weapons. In some countries with strict gun control, this phenomenon is not so evident. However, with the spread of US culture through the entertainment industry, the problem of real-life violence is gradually becoming a problem elsewhere in the world. In the United States, because of limited scientific research on the subject, the National Rifle Association simplistically blames the violent media as the cause of violence in the United States rather than the free access to guns. Some researchers found that there are correlations between playing violent games and self-reported physical fights and delinquent behavior, particularly with greater amounts of time played. Other researchers, however, found that this was only true in a small percentage of children who already exhibited aggressive traits and a high stress level.

Some psychologists speculate that children who are attracted to aggression as a result of watching violent movies or playing violent video games are already prone to aggression in the first place. Other research found that parental involvement—including supervision and support of their children—acts as a deterrent against negative behaviors. The research also found that aggressive kids seem to be drawn to these games, and that these games might have affected them differently from the way they affected kids who were not angry or aggressive. The problem with this research is that it doesn't take into consideration the current state of the family structure, in which supervision and guidance of children is minimal because both parents are at work or the parents are either divorced or separated. And in many cases, the parents are not sufficiently enlightened, especially regarding whether their child is impulsive, aggressive, excessively angry, or possesses other such traits, to have a reasonable input in the child's behavioral development. Furthermore, parents don't have sufficient rights to discipline children because discipline is in many instances considered a form of child abuse.

As discussed earlier, in the absence of quality teaching, the problem will persist, and in the interim, regulation and collaboration between educators and the media regarding the production and distribution of violent media need to take place. Young and immature children cannot tell the difference between reality and fantasy when watching violent movies or cartoons or playing violent video games. According to an Ohio State University study by Elizabeth Armstrong Moore (2012), violent video games and aggression have a negative cumulative effect. Although her study was based on a small sample of seventy participants, it found that people who play violent video games for three consecutive days show increases in aggression and hostility with each day played.

On this cumulative effect, Brad Bushman, the coauthor of the study and a professor of communication and psychology, said, "It could be compared to smoking cigarettes. A single cigarette won't cause lung cancer, but smoking over weeks or months or years greatly increases the risk. In the same way, repeated exposure to violent video games may have a cumulative effect on aggression." Bushman also said, "The results clearly showed that playing a violent video game increases aggressive behavior and also makes people numb to the pain and suffering of others. There is a link between exposure to violent media and violent criminal behavior. We can't do experimental studies. It's just a correlation. Correlation doesn't imply causation, but they're related."

The trouble with the whole debate is that it has been corrupted by those trying to deflect from the harm caused by violent media by using well-adjusted children and teenagers as the social model. This fails to take into consideration that violent media is available to all, including kids with mental illnesses, kids affected by bullying or bullies themselves, and other maladjusted children. Often the talk is focused on the culture of violence that relates only to mass killers. The trouble with society is that it is conditioned to see violence as a part of life and accept it as normal. This social conditioning happens to be the effect of exposure to various forms of media without any form of government regulation on the grounds of free speech. Unfortunately, free speech and lack of censorship don't take into consideration that violence is marketed to vulnerable children and teenagers.

As a diversion from the discussion on the exposure to violent movies and video games, there is another aspect to be considered: adverse environmental factors that can contribute to violent crimes. Factors such as air and water pollution have a direct impact on general health and, more specifically, on mental health. Exposure to lead, for example—as was recently discovered—is directly linked to committing violent crimes. Scientists are starting to find alarming links between children who are exposed to lead and committing violent crime later in life. In the United States, lead is increasingly viewed as a long-term public health risk. Scientists like Sammy Zahran from Columbia University are increasingly looking at lead as a potential cause of impulsive crime. Dr. Zahran said, "I think the true cost of lead, we are only beginning to fully calculate. So this research into violence is only one of a long string of negative outcomes that epidemiologists and economists have noted." In 2012, Dr. Zahran completed a study exploring links between six US cities with high lead pollution and assault rates. He found a consistent twenty-year time gap between lead pollution and violent crime.

Preliminary findings from an Australian study in 2013 also suggest that areas with high lead pollution experience high assault rates at a later date, as lead-exposed children become adults. The Australian study was based on children growing up in close proximity to lead and zinc smelters in the New South Wales town of Boolaroo. In 1991, children at Boolaroo Primary School were given a blood test. Of those children, 84 percent had levels above the maximum allowable of ten micrograms. Professor Mark Taylor, an environmental scientist at Macquarie University of NSW, said, "We know that crime is associated with lower IQ, and we are trying to look at the relationship between the two." His conclusion was that exposure to lead affects children, putting them on a trajectory that, along with other factors in their life, may predispose them to violent activity.

CHAPTER 8

Family Relationships

It's not possible to discuss family relationships without explaining the meaning of altruism and love in the context of marriage, parents, and children. To understand the influences that impact human relationships, it's necessary to separate metaphors from reality, especially the natural element of human selfishness, which is glossed over by social conditioning and, in turn, by social commentators. This is mainly caused by the adoption in daily human relations of an idealistic religious perspective and philosophy at the expense of the more realistic evolutionary observations. For stable human relationships to exist, societies need to accept that the survival instinct of a person has an element of selfishness and that the best way to deal with this fact is not by adopting so-called absolute altruism as a main mission but by adopting and promoting the principles of give-and-take and win-win against the winner-takes-all principle.

About altruism generally, it should be asked: What causes people to jeopardize their own health and well-being to help other people? What is it that inspires individuals to give their time, energy, and money to aid in the betterment of others, even when they receive nothing tangible or intangible in return? Altruism involves the unselfish concern for other people. It involves doing things simply out of a desire to help, not because one feels obligated to out of duty, loyalty, or religious reasons.

As for love and marriage, which are the other parts of family relationships, the subject is dealt with on a journey into evolutionary psychology about mating, intelligence, creativity, personality, and cultural psychology.

Altruism

Some sociologists define altruism as instinctive total devotion and attention to others, when empathy (which makes humans successful social animals) is strongest, with full focus of emotion on someone. Individuals' emotions and interest in others differ to a great degree in different relationships, including the bond between mother and child.

Other sociologists define altruism as the principle or practice of unselfish concern for or devotion to the welfare of others, which is the opposite of egoism. And generosity is when acting with an unselfish regard for others doesn't always come naturally but through social conditioning. Some psychologists believe that we're hardwired for empathy, since cooperative behavior allowed our ancestors to survive under harsh conditions. And most of us realize that when we make the effort to give without expectations of reciprocity, we feel fulfilled and energized. Other psychologists classify empathy as a behavior that is prosocial, which means that it benefits other people, no matter the motive or how the giver benefits.

The majority of psychologists believe that altruism exists for biological, neurological, and cognitive reasons. The biological reason, or kin selection, causes a person to be more altruistic toward his or her blood relations in order to increase the chances of the survival of future generations. The neurological reason relates to the activation of reward centers in the brain and is based on the theory that when a person engages in an altruistic act, the pleasure centers of the brain become active. The cognitive reason relates to the definition of altruism that states that the incentive to do for others without reward could be a response to relieve one's own distress or simply to be kind to others out of empathy.

> **Warning:** The following discussion could be a bit tedious and confusing to some readers. When you feel so inclined, please skip this part and go to "Realistic Altruism" below.

In the study of social evolution, altruism refers to behavior by an individual that increases the fitness of another individual while decreasing the fitness of the actor. Or, according to the *International Encyclopedia of the Social Sciences* (2008), psychological altruism is "a motivational state with the goal of increasing another's welfare."

On the other hand is the social-exchange theory. This theory states that "altruism can only exist when benefits outweigh costs, which means altruism doesn't work when there is a lack of external rewards for altruistic behavior."

Finally, there is the kin-selection theory, based on observation of animals and humans, which is confirmed in many studies of different cultures. It concludes that "one is more altruistic toward close kin than to distant kin and non-kin. Even subtle cues indicating kinship may unconsciously increase altruistic behavior."

In evolutionary biology, an organism is said to behave altruistically when its behavior benefits other organisms at a cost to itself. The costs and benefits are measured in terms of *reproductive fitness*, or expected number of offspring. So by behaving altruistically, an organism reduces the number of offspring it is likely to produce itself but boosts the number that other organisms are likely to produce. This biological notion of altruism is not identical to the everyday concept. In everyday parlance, an action would only be called "altruistic" if it was done with the conscious intention of helping another. But in the biological sense, there is no such requirement. Some of the most interesting examples of biological altruism are found among creatures that are (presumably) not capable of conscious thought (e.g., insects). For the biologist, it is the consequences of an action for reproductive fitness that determine whether the action counts as altruistic, not the intentions, if any, with which the action is performed.

From an earlier Darwinian viewpoint, natural selection leads us to expect animals to behave in ways that increase their *own* chances of survival and reproduction, not those of others. But by behaving altruistically, an animal reduces its own fitness, putting itself at a selective disadvantage to the one that behaves selfishly. For example, when observing danger, most animals sound the alarm, but selfishly some don't, and the latter end up benefiting from the alarm calls of others. In this instance, natural selection favors those animals that do not give alarm calls over those that do.

Therefore, based on earlier Darwinian conclusion, a group containing lots of altruists, each ready to subordinate their own interests for the greater good of the group, has a survival advantage over a group composed mainly of selfish animals. This process is driven by the instinct of the survival of the species. Groups composed only or mainly of selfish animals become extinct.

However, the idea that group selection might explain the evolution of altruism was negated by Darwin himself when he realized that "he who was ready to sacrifice his life, as many a savage has been, rather than betray his comrades, would often leave no offspring to inherit his noble nature." He suggested that self-sacrificial behavior, though disadvantageous for the individual member of a tribe, might be beneficial at the group level. A tribe always ready to give aid to each other and sacrifice themselves for the common good would be victorious over most other tribes; this would be natural selection.

According to Richard Dawkins, the major weakness of group selection as an explanation of altruism is that it ignores the "subversion from within" element. Dawkins says, "Even if altruism is advantageous at the group level, within any group, altruists are liable to be exploited by selfish 'free-riders' who refrain from behaving altruistically. These free-riders will have an obvious fitness advantage: they benefit from the altruism of others, but do not incur any of the costs. So even if a group is composed exclusively of altruists, all behaving nicely toward each other, it only takes a single selfish mutant to bring an end to this happy idyll. By virtue of its relative fitness advantage within the group, the selfish mutant will out-reproduce the altruists; hence selfishness will eventually swamp altruism." Therefore, the "subversion within" theory is regarded as a major problem for the group-altruism evolution theorists to answer.

Realistic Altruism

For the modern social structure (based on social-exchange theory), the above confused definitions don't tell the full story of the human psyche, especially the psychological reward or the other expected reward from an altruistic act. This can be seen when people ignore the need of others in distress. The display of coldheartedness not only relates to cultural conditioning but also to our primitive nature. Nature equipped humans and other species with the instinct to exchange empathy—to share pleasure and distress signals. The reproductive success of the species relates to the mutual instinct of compassion and self-preservation. Accordingly, it is the exchange element that drives the successful and harmonious human relations and the concept of altruism.

The idea of the existence of the reward element in altruism is usually disputed or dismissed on cultural and religious grounds. This is because we are biblically and idealistically conditioned to blindly believe in the scripture, and it is heresy to think otherwise. Religious upbringing covers up, or at least doesn't take into consideration, the fact that our social and religious prejudices often prevent us from acting altruistically. Consider our response (or the lack thereof) to situations in which our sympathy for and help of others—especially strangers—is desperately needed. During many events in which our attention, empathy, and emotional connection are in demand, they are shut down by our social divide. This generally happens when no emotional reward is anticipated. Sometimes the Samaritan in us subconsciously gets the satisfaction or the expectation of the eventual recognition for his or her act. In most cases, the element of reward exists, including the exchange of affection between a mother and her child. The mutual satisfaction derived from this exchange is a great motivation for the mother's full devotion and emotional connection to her child. The child's offer of his or her affection to the mother stems from his or her survival instinct.

The survival-of-the-fittest instinct equips a person with the desire to eliminate competitors, including his or her own siblings; this instinct is often curbed through social conditioning. However, when the ultimate survival of someone is under threat, the law of the jungle takes over. As is often seen during African famines, when a mother has a choice to feed and save only one child instead of her other six children, she chooses the fittest child to survive and lets the other six die. This is the cruelty of nature that demonstrates the contradiction in human instincts.

The other aspect of altruism is social reciprocation, which is mostly driven by cultural and religious considerations. In a normal social setting, altruism is based on the expectation of giving and taking, which is part of the human nature of selfishness when the expectation of loving someone entails being loved in return. It's the individual's need that dictates his or her behavior. One's needs are the main drivers of emotions. The mutual principle applies; that is, when you recognize someone, for example, you expect to be recognized in return. And when you care for someone, you expect to be cared for in return. This includes caring for your offspring now so they may care for you later, which is a human tendency that to date is still prevalent in countries where no social security or safety net exists.

Ultimately, reciprocal altruism and selfishness are the same, despite the fact that some idealists try to make people feel guilty for being selfish. Idealists promote the unnatural concept of absolute altruism and blind sacrifice as the main human mission. This applies to religion that teaches people the virtues of absolute, unconditional giving, and sacrificing based on the assumption that God gave and sacrificed; it doesn't take into consideration the human nature of selfishness and that the absolute doesn't exist. It is obvious that the religious philosophy of unconditional giving is an unnatural and out-of-date ethical teaching that didn't work in the past and will not work in the future. The dogma of giving and sacrificing can only help religious establishments to grow richer and more powerful at the expense of the indoctrinated followers who have been conditioned only to give. It's a dogma designed to benefit the church at the expense of its followers. Since its inception, religion has affected human perception, distorted and confused social psychology, exploited human emotions, and caused conflicts, especially through the different interpretations of the so-called holy books and their revelations. It has had a negative impact on human relations, both within communities and globally.

Reciprocation, on the other hand, and the adoption of give-and-take and win-win principles provide a better foundation for human relations. These principles are more in tune with human nature than the failed religious teachings of unconditional giving and sacrificing. Give-and-take and win-win are more realistic as materialistic principles and more applicable to human relations than the selfless and sacrificial ones. The collapse of communism because of the minimal incentive given to people to produce for a reasonable material reward, rather than a moral one, could be a good example of tangible and intangible human needs. The promotion of individuality on the basis that humans are selfish might be the correct course for humanity's progress and could result in a more harmonious society than the religiously fragmented and conflicted one.

Accordingly, it could be necessary for the world to get rid of the historic indoctrination strategy that created conflict as a result of the subjective ideologies and conformity, which was imposed by manipulative social, political, and religious leaders. To create a more harmonious world, new leaders and philosophers are desperately needed to rid the world of the impractical idealism of absolutes. This is not meant to change the world drastically, but to get rid of religious idealism, fear, guilt, and the practice of mass psychology and indoctrination, all of which inhibit creativity and individuality.

Changing the world drastically may necessitate the elimination of all religions. And in the current circumstances, when illiteracy and ignorance are still rife, this is impractical and difficult to achieve. Many civilized countries, however, are well overdue for shedding the outdated religious philosophies of idealism. In the interim, through secular education, the attitude of unconditional giving and sacrificing could be taught as a secondary principle to balance the needs of civilization in the transitional phase of eliminating ignorance until science takes total hold. For a civilized transition to the total scientific world, more moderate, realistic, and more scientifically oriented religious leaders are needed to replace the currently dominant and extreme, ultraconservative ones.

Love and Marriage

When discussing emotional and social intelligences, some psychologists focus their attention on the success of marriage and place undue emphasis on love while ignoring the simple fact that over 50 percent of marriages are followed by separation, divorce, or disharmony. Other psychologists reach misleading conclusions based on a sample of interviewees that mainly represents the middle class and fails to take into consideration the diversity of society. Further, their samples are often based on participants from a selective social group in a selective environment that doesn't account for dynamic social change. In many instances, social change occurs in the majority/minority or high migrations ratios—countries like the United States, Canada, and Australia—and in relation to the degree of women's liberation, achievements, participation in work, and degree of economic independence.

The culture and the expectations in marriages have altered dramatically. A century ago, when the man was the only provider, the role of women was more defined; a couple married for keeps in a union that established a close-knit family. The family obeyed a religious moral code, and the economy and society were designed for passing on wealth between generations. Marriage then was based on "till death do us part."

In the secular society of the twenty-first century, where women are liberated and individuality and independence are the main elements of relationships, marriage is now driven by false romantic hopes and physical attraction. It is influenced by Hollywood instead of being founded on a soul-mate basis. Furthermore, modern marriage, with its notion of equality of the sexes and of being all things to each other, is totally different from the marriages of past generations that were based on gender hierarchy. The elements of hardship of past generations versus the prosperity of younger generations made the expectations in relationships totally different. Above all, the easy modern life is producing a generation that easily succumbs to disappointment and negativity in the event of a setback or adversity. This problem is highlighted by the high rate of divorce of young couples compared to the much lower rate of divorce of past generations, when couples also married very early and well before maturity.

However, some marriages today are starting later in life than those of the older generations. Being more mature and more financially secure before marriage, the younger generation gains some advantages in the decision-making process. The divorce rate in older generations is increasing, especially after the children leave home. This is occurring because partners were staying together for the sake of children; women are more financially secure, more educated, and more confident. For an increasing number of long-term marriages, it's no longer a case of "till death do us part;" it's a matter of until the children depart from the family nest.

A report in 2013, entitled *"Working Out Relationships,"* by the Australian Institute of Family Studies has found a sharp increase in the number of couples calling it quits after twenty years of marriage. Those who have children eighteen years and younger seem to be less likely to divorce, but once the children leave the nest, couples reevaluate and reprioritize. The wife is now more likely to initiate divorce, which is a sign of women's increasing economic and personal independence. Another contributing factor is longevity, which discourages couples from staying together for many more years. Furthermore, social attitudes toward divorce have changed, and it no longer carries the negative stigma of the old days.

The modern age is characterized by the disintegration of the concept of family as an institution and the diminishment of religious influence. Young people are growing up as individuals rather than as obedient conformists. At the same time, education lacks the teaching methods to compensate for the huge social gap caused by these facts. Accordingly, society is saddled with huge problems, especially the disadvantaged, neglected, and poorly educated children, who need a major adjustment to avoid a major social upheaval. Politicians are busy with their self-serving tactics and driving the country into divisiveness and polarization, instead of paying deserving attention to the brewing social problems. The problem is on an escalating trajectory and in desperate need of a high-priority bipartisan approach. To avoid the deepening of social harm, a solution could be found within the education system.

Family trouble now stems from the idea that we seek perfection in a partner. We want one relationship to give us everything, including romantic euphoria, perfect children, plenty of money, and great orgasms. When these expectations are dashed, disappointment sets in, and the relationship becomes burdensome and often ends up collapsing. This is when the partners forget that both biologically and socially, men and women are different, and nature intended for them to have different roles and to complete each other. Their complementary roles are biologically enshrined in the survival instincts, which should not be corrupted by other considerations. For a relationship to survive—before and after marriage—it should be based on the concept of needing each other rather than on the fantasy of love and altruism, because love and altruism are not durable commodities compared to other tangible and intangible human needs. Marriage should also be based on the understanding that nobody is perfect and everybody is different, especially today, when individuality is triumphing over conformism.

The problem with marriages is aggravated by the lack of emotional and social intelligences. This includes not understanding that the initial romantic euphoria is a passing phase that is far removed from the reality of life. Falling in love is a short-term hormonal-biological affair that is in conflict with the long-term requirement of family relationships. **Falling in love*** is generally driven by the first look and physical attraction, followed by an attempt to impress the other by displaying perfect behavior and pretending that we are more than what we really are. Beauty has some role in the attraction, but self-confidence and self-awareness—the core elements of personality—play a huge role in sexual attraction. It's appropriate here to sound a warning that a person who pretends and projects an exaggerated or pompous personality is generally boring and cannot live up to expectations and ends up exposed as phony, with his or her relationship doomed. And the person who places too much emphasis on physical appearance can expect huge competition from other hunters. In addition, he or she should be aware that in the long term, one's physical look changes—with age and diet or bearing children or drinking too much beer. Worse yet, when intellectual conversation becomes mundane and when routine and boredom set in, the other side of one's personality and bad habits comes to the fore. This is when the majority who build their relationships on false premises and false images cannot face reality and end up either divorced or living in disharmony. Accordingly, many adults are not suitable for marriage and more so for having children. A family living in disharmony or divorce causes children to suffer for no fault of their own, and ultimately society bears the brunt.

*** Falling in love** *is generally based on possessiveness. Pretending to belong to each other is a cover-up for reality that is based on the principle of ownership. This can be observed during the early courtship of partners, which is full of manipulation and acting. The manipulative process is hidden behind the pretention to be altruistic, when it could be said that each partner is planning to have future advantages and ultimate domination over the other. When the plan fails and domination doesn't succeed, the reality changes to the detriment of the relationship. The process of manipulation in the early stages of a relationship can be observed by partners going out of their way to avoid displaying their bad habits and the ugly side of their personality. Their initial motive is to* **hook or get hooked***.*

When the hormonal euphoria that is associated with romance and the harmonious rhythm dies, the hidden personality appears, and the disappointment starts. After marriage, some couples begin to take each other for granted, and often the essential elements of attraction get neglected, such as personal hygiene, affection, common purpose, and so on.

People forget that at a young age, physical attributes play a major role in a relationship, but at an older age, the relationship is based on emotional attributes and the need for partnership. People also forget that in any relationship, there are advantages and disadvantages, and negatives and positives. When the focus is on the negatives and the disadvantages, the relationship is doomed. On the other hand, the relationship can survive and prosper when the focus is on the positives and the advantages. In every scenario, emotional intelligence plays the starring role. The application of the win-win principle can be the key to avoiding conflicts. Above all, people forget that falling in love is a selfish act; if it didn't suit the person, he or she wouldn't consider love worth going through its long-term agony for the short-term ecstasy. Because of our social conditioning, however, many idealists might refute this proposition. We are religiously taught to accept the absolute love and altruism as one of the main human missions.

However, with self-awareness and awareness of others, a better outcome can be achieved. Here and yet again, it is necessary to highlight the most important aspect of personal success in marriage and in life generally, which is the development of emotional intelligence as a first step toward understanding others. Dr. Daniel Goleman—mentioned earlier—in his book, *Emotional Intelligence*, (2006), wrote,

The current trends in marriage and divorce make emotional intelligence more crucial than ever...Consider divorce rates. The rate *per year* of divorces has more or less levelled off. But there is another way of calculating divorce rates, one that suggests a perilous climb: looking at the odds that a given newly married couple will have their marriage *eventually* end in divorce. Although the overall rate of divorce has stopped climbing, the risk of divorce has been shifting to newlyweds.

From statistical analysis he concludes the following:

Since 1970, newlyweds had a fifty/fifty chance of splitting up or staying together. And for married couples starting out in 1990, the likelihood that the marriage would end in divorce was projected to be close to a staggering 67 percent. This makes the emotional forces between husband and wife much more crucial for the survival of their marriage.

To improve relationships, it's worth referring to Dr. John Gottman's book, *The Relationship Cure: A 5 Step Guide to Strengthening Your Marriage, Family, and Friendships*, (2002), in which he provides a practical program for transforming troubled relationships into positive ones. His five steps can help you build a better emotional connection with your partner and other people you care about. His simple five-step program is based on twenty years of research on how to improve all personal relationships, including those between husband and wife or with lovers, children, and colleagues. He adopts the concept of emotional bids (emotional exchanges or emotional dealings) on how to short-circuit personal connection and communication. Gottman gives good practical advice and provides examples of wrong and right ways to deal and interact with aggressive or passive partners and others. His five-step program mainly consists of the following:

- Analyze the way you bid emotionally and the way you respond to others' emotional bids.
- Discover how your brain's emotional command systems affect your bidding process.
- Examine how your emotional heritage impacts your ability to connect with others and your style of bidding.
- Develop your emotional communication skills.
- Find shared meaning with others.

In his other book, *The Seven Principles for Making Marriage Work*, (2000), Gottman outlines the principles of how to teach partners new strategies for making their marriage work. He analyzes the bad habits of married couples and establishes a method of correcting the behaviors that destroy marriages. He helps couples focus on each other and learn how to become soul mates. Briefly, his seven principles are as follows:

- Enhance your love maps.
- Nurture your fondness and admiration.
- Turn toward each other instead of away.
- Let your partner influence you.
- Solve your solvable problems.
- Overcome gridlock.
- Create shared meaning.

No matter what, however, in any relationship one partner will always have more influence than the other in a specific decision. The dominance of one partner depends on the matter to be decided on, whether it is about food, money, shopping, entertainment, traveling, and so on. Subtle negotiation of the role rather than forcefulness is the ideal approach. Forcefulness will provoke conflict, which can escalate into anger and insult. Talking over each other creates an uneasy feeling. An emotionally intelligent partner should be able to attune to the feeling of the other with an understanding of how to pacify and achieve a better outcome. A partner with a sense of humor and a good feel for timing is an ideal partner. A serious and pompous partner who takes himself or herself too seriously is destined to be a boring partner and should be avoided at all costs.

An essential element in a partnership is the ability to respect and accept oneself as basically good. This relates to a person's ability to feel fulfilled and satisfied with himself or herself regardless of perceived strengths and weaknesses and, to a great extent, determines a person's levels of self-assuredness, self-esteem, and self-respect. As discussed earlier, another essential element for the survival of a partnership is focusing on the positives instead of the negatives. Because we are brought up differently and our perceptions are different, the positives and the negatives will always be present and relative. Therefore, it should be remembered that focusing on the negatives can cause any relationship to be doomed.

As for loyalty—in marriage and in life generally—it leads to giving partners peace of mind, which is an essential element of trust. Generally, a partner may only demand loyalty if he or she can offer the same in return. The same applies to being committed to each other. In both cases, mutual efforts and being conscious of the facts are essential elements for a durable relationship. Equality in marriage is achieved when one marries an equal partner; otherwise, inequality should be expected. Before one builds a high expectation for equality, other factors should be taken into consideration, especially the country's cultural aspects. Generally, culture develops by evolution at a slow pace, which makes cultural revolution an impractical goal to aspire to.

A solid relationship in any culture demands the ability for timing of a discussion on any serious family matter to avoid distraction and argument. Timing can also lead to avoiding emotional outbursts and can make it easier to find a solution or an alternative to any contentious issue.

Again, here it is necessary to emphasize the importance of emotional intelligence for dealing with family problems, which helps in applying different techniques for changing thinking and behavior.

Emotional intelligence equips individuals to have a more relaxed approach and the ability to pacify others when there is a potential for argument. It equips the person with self-control—thinking and listening before acting—and improves his or her communication skills. Above all, it stops the individual from projecting a destructive false image that is driven by insecurity or an inferiority complex.

Money and Marriage

Unfortunately, money is one of the destructive weapons of marriages. Statistically, partners fight about money much more than they argue about sex. In fact, these issues often start before marriage. Even when both partners work and earn money, they don't always agree on financial issues.

Such a scenario may seem fair if the partners share all family expenses and then keep or spend what is left to suit each of them. But even this simple and fair formula can be a cause of resentment. Personality and power play are at the center of most conflict between partners. Here the conflict is between spenders or savers, earning more or earning less, being domineering or not, and being more selfish or less. The conflict is exacerbated by lack of communication and cooperation between partners.

The projection of a false image before marriage usually comes back to haunt a person—especially if power play is behind it—as it is a sign of dishonesty in the relationship. To avoid the disappointment and resentment that lead to stress and tension during married life, honesty from the start of dating is essential. This is true for success not only in marriage but in life generally. Honesty leads to better communication, and money matters between couples become a nonissue.

Research shows that money is one of the main reasons couples fight and is a main cause of divorce. Yet most couples do not talk about money before they marry. Before marriage, for some reason, couples talk about sex more than they talk about money. This may be because sex is seen as an immediate natural priority. Couples in the early stages of dating are preoccupied with sweeping each other off their feet and may forget or be ashamed to discuss money matters. Unfortunately, soon after marriage, when they establish a joint bank account, it becomes clear that there is a problem on the horizon. Carried by the momentum, they continue with their spending habits until the problem brings things to a halt and the trouble starts. Worse still is when the credit card is in debt after the family is formed with two or more children to be fed and one of the partners out of work. This is the time for a reality check and the discovery that romance and money don't mix. And this is why 50 percent of divorces are the result of money matters. According to Dr. Arthur Aron, a social psychologist at Stony Brook University, "Part of the reason for the disconnect from reality may be because we are hard-wired to ignore practical concerns in the throes of romance." Dr. Aron also said, "Romantic love usually wears off in one to four years."

As can be seen, romantic love is a luxury in any partnership, and money can ruin a marriage. A family is a business partnership in which both partners must play a part. As in any failed business partnership, the lesson learned from the first encounter is not repeated in the next. Before one marries for the second time, financial vigilance and compatibility become the priority rather than blind romance. Above all, pretension and the projection of a false personality become things of the past.

Those in the process of romancing with a view to marrying and starting a family should consider the following elementary:

- Money doesn't grow on trees, and substantial debt is a marriage killer.
- The romance will fade away soon after marriage. Emotions don't overcome money troubles, and money doesn't buy love (although to some, it does).
- A big and expensive fairy-tale wedding to impress families and friends is the wrong way to start a marriage. It's commercially driven and designed to deceive yourself and others. An extravaganza of a wedding could even indicate a personality disorder of insecurity and narcissism, especially the show-off syndrome.

- Each partner should have some financial freedom in the partnership, but this freedom must be used with accountability within the family budget.
- Financial freedom starts with separate bank accounts.
- Partners should understand that it is a cardinal mistake to live beyond their means.
- Communication and agreement are a must.
- Financial ignorance can lead to ruin.
- Above all, remember that a divorce can have a devastating effect on the children.

Sex and Marriage

Warning: Please note that the following contains some material suitable only for adults.

After your arduous journey through this book, it's time to wind down and let your hair down. It's time to discuss this interesting topic with those of you who consider sex a natural escapade. It's understandable that some other readers, especially the very serious ones, may find the following discussion a bit distasteful, and it may prejudice them against the book. I know that while the uninhibited readers view sex as a natural act and treat it with honesty, others may consider it a taboo subject. It's my view that since sex is at the center of marriage, it should be treated with honesty and without excessive inhibition. I care about what you think, but I feel the book is incomplete without exploring it.

In addition, at the end of the book, I've included some naughty (but relevant) jokes about sex in marriage, and this may disappoint some of you. Please forgive me if you do not find them to your liking. Remember, there is no writer in the world that can please everyone.

First the serious part:

In their book *Mating Intelligence Unleashed: The Role of the Mind in Sex, Dating, and Love*, (2013), psychologists Dr. Glenn Geher (the founder of NorthEastern Evolutionary Psychology Society) and Scott Barry Kaufman, his cofounder of International Evolutionary Studies, describe human mating as instinctual. They describe courtship as a display of sexual competition and rivalry that requires a range of mental abilities evolved to help people find the right partner. Their book, about mating and intelligence, is a journey into evolutionary psychology, intelligence, creativity, personality, and social psychology. It confirms that physical attractiveness isn't the only factor in mating. Mating also includes mental skills, charisma, sense of humor, creativity, and a bit of feeling. The book also explains the role of personality in mating, the role of deception in manipulation, and, most importantly, the role of emotional intelligence. Boys and girls learn emotions and their meanings differently. To have each other, initially they act differently and have different expectations that eventually contradict their own realities. This leads to different physical and emotional outcomes.

The biological and psychological makeups of men and women are different. Their sexual desire mostly depends on two major factors, hormones and social conditioning. Because of the historical patriarchal role played by man, his libido became mostly dependent on hormonal factors, while the woman's secondary and domestic role resulted in her libido becoming mostly conditional. This could be one of the reasons women depend more on foreplay and emotional stimulus for their arousal, while the man's arousal is generally automatic. Other reasons a woman might not enjoy sex could be that her partner no longer turns her on or is no longer capable of pleasing her sexually. It is estimated that 40 percent of women never have an orgasm from intercourse with a partner. The reason men want sex more than women do is not about differing levels of desire; unlike women, men have almost a 100 percent guarantee of physical pleasure and satisfaction through orgasm. It should be taken into consideration that even though a woman does not always reach orgasm, she often derives total psychological satisfaction from the man's orgasm. This could be more so when a couple is living harmoniously and affectionately. Otherwise, to pretend that she is normal or to satisfy her and her man's psychological egos, the woman would fake an orgasm.

Maintaining a long-term sexual relationship in a marriage is not easy, even for healthy and well-connected couples. It requires time and intimacy. Hectic daily life presents major challenges, such as work, children, money, worries, and so on.

These daily routines of life—whether careers, children, or financial responsibilities, which are complicated further by aging, heart problems, depression, and so on—affect the physical conditions that can have a negative impact on sex. However, in a psychologically mature relationship, sex can be a pressure-release mechanism in adverse conditions.

It stands to reason that if men do more or the same amount of housework, such as cooking, cleaning, and looking after the kids, their libido will be more moderate. Western society is now in a transitional mode; women are achieving gradual economic and psychological equality with men, and this in turn has an impact on women's approach to sex. Woman's liberation is giving women more confidence to demand equality, both physical and emotional. They are now less inhibited than in the past. In the old days, for example, it was natural for the man to be on top during the sex act (the missionary position), but now the woman is assuming a new role and exploring different positions.

A marriage is a happy beginning to many things. But when it comes to sex, marriage can do more damage than good. Sex is a wonderful thing until it becomes routine, after the novelty of the new marriage wears off. This is especially the case when sex is always available and partners live and spend most of their free time together. These factors affect the libido and ultimately the frequency of sex, which in many instances leads to frustration. And instead of serving as an opportunity to develop intimacy, spare time becomes filled with arguments and nagging.

Sex is very personal and means different things to different people. For some, sex is to be shared only with someone close and intimate. For others, it can be with anyone. From a religious perspective, sex is only part of the **chastity of marriage*** that is based on the theology of the body, which is a God-created expression of marital love and openness to new life that contributes to the holiness of the couple. According to Catholic catechism, "The call to holiness in marriage is a lifelong process of conversion and growth."

* **Chastity of marriage:** *The Church defines chastity as "the successful integration of sexuality within the person." Married couples practice the conjugal (wedded life) chastity that is proper to their state in life.*

Unfortunately, the church has no definition for the chastity of its pedophile priests.

The other aspect of sex and marriage is infidelity, a human tendency that some consider one of the secrets of a marriage's longevity. It follows the doctrine that variety is the spice of life. However, in an unstable marriage, infidelity becomes addictive and destructive. Despite its attractiveness, happily married couples avoid it at all costs, and they should.

Now the naughty part:

To have more fun about sex in marriage (or maybe not), I'm listing below some relevant jokes from my book, *Dads Gags*, (2009). (Be warned, you may find some of the jokes a bit naughty.)

God breathed life into Adam and told him, "You are Man, my most favored creation; because of this I am going to give you the penis and the brain."

Adam replied, "Thank you, Lord. Thank you so much—thank you."

God said, "Don't get too excited—there is a catch."

"What's the catch?" Adam asked.

God replied, "You're not going to be able to use both of them at the same time."

☺

Before marriage, women should know that the man has two brains, one on top and one in the middle. The one on top is a twisted thinker, and the one in the middle is a straight thinker.

☺

Marriage is when a man and woman become one; the trouble starts when they try to decide which one.

☺

A doctor examining a woman who had been rushed to the emergency room took her husband aside and said, "I don't like the look of your wife at all."

"Me neither, Doc," said the husband. "But she is a great cook and a very good mother to the kids."

On the night of their wedding, a young couple retired to their hotel suite. After making her final preparations for bed, the bride came out of the bathroom to find her groom kneeling. "What are you doing, darling?" she asked.

"I'm praying for guidance," he said.

"I'll take care of the guidance," she said. "And you better pray for stamina."

The morning after their wedding night, the husband got up early, went to the kitchen, and brought his wife a nice breakfast in bed. She was delighted with his gesture, and he asked her if she was happy with what he'd done. "Of course, dear," she replied. "Everything is perfect."

He said, "Good. This is the way I want my breakfast served every day."

Man's perfect woman:

- She must be beautiful.
- She must be considerate.
- She must be economical.
- She must be good in bed.
- She must be a good cook.

Unfortunately, the law doesn't allow more than one wife.

Woman's perfect man:

- He must help around the house.
- He must make you laugh.
- He must be able to count.
- He must enjoy making love to you.
- He must not be a liar.

It is important that these five men don't know each other.

☺

In the first year of marriage, the man speaks, and the woman listens.

In the second year, the woman speaks, and the man listens.

In the third year, they both speak, and the neighbors listen.

Billy walks into the kitchen, looks at his wife, and says, "My God, your ass is getting as big as a barbeque."

That night they are in bed, and he is getting frisky.

She turns to him and says, "If you think that I am going to fire up the barbeque for one little sausage, then you must be crazy."

Claire was enrolled in nursing school and was attending anatomy class. The subject that day was involuntary muscles. The instructor, who was hoping to stimulate the students a bit, asked Claire if she knew what her arse-hole did when she had an orgasm.

"Sure!" she said, "He was at home looking after the kids!"

☺

Joe asks his wife about what to give her on their wedding anniversary.

"Would you like a new mink coat?" he asks.

"Not really," says Karen.

"Well, how about a new sports car?" says Joe.

"No," she responds.

"What about a new holiday home?" he suggests.

She again rejects his offer with a "No thanks."

"Well, what *would* you like for our anniversary?" asks Joe.

"Darling, I would like a divorce," answers Karen.

Joe replies, "Sorry, I wasn't planning to spend that much money."

An American, an Australian, and an Irishman were in a pub discussing the mental abilities of their blonde wives.

The American said, "You know, my wife must be the stupidest woman in the world. She went to a supermarket sale and bought five hundred dollars' worth of meat, and we don't even have a freezer."

The Australian said, "That is nothing, mates! My wife went to a showroom and bought a brand-new car, and she doesn't even have a driver's license."

Not to be outdone, the Irishman said, "Oh, my wife is so much dumber than that! Last week she left for a holiday to Tahiti with a pack of twelve condoms! Hell, she doesn't even have a penis."

Speaking of the penis, it is a popular yet controversial organ to talk or write about. It's an organ that has baffled scientists for centuries, and still no one can completely understand it. It's an organ used for pleasure, making children, and socializing. And when it raises its head, it is the sign of health and happiness. Researchers support the hypothesis that penis size partly evolved because of female choice when everything was on show before humans wore clothing. Penis size may be a hormonal signal or something nice to look at. Fortunately, woman selects her mate not by the size of his penis, but for other physical and psychological qualities. Equally, man selects a woman not by the size of her breasts or her height, but for her personality.

Happy marriage, ladies and gentlemen, and till death do you part!

ACKNOWLEDGMENTS

Psychology as a science and a philosophy was developed over many centuries, but it's still the subject of continuous research and disputes. Considering the complexity of the information processed by the brain, we can say that research on the brain and its wirings is still in its infancy. This leads to many problems in the literature of and about the discipline. Some psychologists use figurative language and speculation instead of undisputed scientific facts. Further, psychology has developed into a scientific discipline, complete with heavy use of technical terminology. Readers must constantly reach for a dictionary to understand psychological texts, which makes reading burdensome. And sometimes the technical terms used are not even mentioned in traditional dictionaries. Often psychologists give the impression that they are talking with one another rather than with general readers. Some psychologists even base their arguments on pseudoscience, especially when explaining consciousness as a global collective related to galactic events such as energy pulses from a black hole in the Milky Way or solar-flare cycles from the sun. Some others use unscientific expressions as a substitute for facts when dealing with the scientific aspects of psychology.

However, there are just as many psychologists and writers who try to simplify and demystify the subject for the general reader, many of whom I have grown to admire for their solid and comprehensible work. In writing this book, I am following in their footsteps. One of those psychologists and writers is Daniel Goleman, whose clarity of writing, especially on the subjects of emotional and social intelligences, cannot be disputed. Howard Gardner's writing, although it is a bit complicated—written by a psychologist for other psychologists—has made a huge contribution to modernizing the subject. Gardner's knowledge and approach were a huge inspiration for me to write and simplify the text of basic psychology. Others who made huge contributions to the subject and our enlightenment are Peter Salovey, Reuven Bar-On, David Caruso, and John Mayer. On the subject of intelligence and IQ, the work of Philip Carter is essential reading, especially for educators and parents. Also valuable is the work on mental disorders by Steven Zarit and Judy Zarit and the work of Peter K. Smith on the subject of bullying at school. On human relations and family relationships generally, I admire the work of Glenn Geher and John Gottman. Last is Virgil Ziegler-Hill for his work on the subject of narcissism.

This book is dedicated to these writers and scholars and to the people who are motivated to improve their self-understanding and their understanding of their social environment, especially those who can dig deep into the subconscious to resolve their common personality disorders.

Finally, I wish to extend my thanks and appreciation to the CreateSpace team for their excellent work and professionalism, especially in the editing and the production of this book.

REFERENCES

Encyclopedia Britannica

Encyclopedia Microsoft Encarta

Encyclopedia of Applied Psychology

International Encyclopedia of Social Sciences

Wikipedia

The Bible–The Old and the New Testaments

Bar-On, Reuven and James Parker. *The Handbook of Emotional Intelligence: Theory, Development, Assessment, and Application at Home, School and in the Workplace.* San Francisco, CA: Jossey-Bass, 2000.

Bar-On, Reuven and Maurice Elias. *Educating People to Be Emotionally Intelligent.* Westport, CT: Praeger, 2007.

Carter, Philip. *IQ and Psychometric Test Workbook: Essential Preparation for Verbal, Numerical and Spatial*

Aptitude Tests and Personality Tests. Rev. ed. London: Kogan Page, 2011.

———. *IQ and Aptitude Tests: Assess Your Verbal, Numerical and Spatial Reasoning Skills*. Rev. edition. London: Kogan Page, 2011.

Elias, Maurice, Steven Tobias, and Brian Friedlander. *Raising Emotionally Intelligent Teenagers: Guiding the Way for Compassionate, Committed, Courageous Adults*. New York: Three Rivers, 2000.

Gardner, Howard. *Multiple Intelligence: New Horizons in Theory and Practice*. Reprint. New York: Basic Books, 2006.

———. *Intelligence Reframed: Multiple Intelligences for the 21st Century*. New York: Basic Books, 2000.

Gardner, Howard and Hatch, Thomas. "Multiple Intelligences Go to School: Educational Implication of the Theory of Multiple Intelligences." *Journal of Educational Researcher*. American Educational Research Association, US: 1989.

Geher, Glen, Scott Barry Kaufman, and Helen Fisher. *Mating Intelligence Unleashed: The Role of the Mind in Sex, Dating, and Love*. USA: Oxford University Press, 2013.

Goleman, Daniel. *Emotional Intelligence*. 10th anniversary edition. New York: Bantam Books, 2006.

————. *Social Intelligence: The New Science of Human Relationships*. Reprint. New York: Bantam Books, 2007.

Gottman John. *The Relationship Cure: A 5 Step Guide to Strengthening Your Marriage, Family, and Friendships*. Reprint. New York: Three Rivers, 2002.

Gottman, John and Joan Declaire. *Raising an Emotionally Intelligent Child: The Heart of Parenting*. New York: Simon & Schuster.1998.

Gottman, John and Nan Silver. *The Seven Principles for Making Marriage Work*. New York: Orion Publishing Group, 2000.

Kernberg, Otto. *Borderline Conditions and Pathological Narcissism*. Maryland: The Rowman & Littlefield Publishers, Inc., 1992.

Mayer, Erin and Virgil Zeigler-Hill. "How Much Do Narcissists Really Like Themselves?" *Elsevier Journal of Research in Personality*. West Carolina and Rochester Universities, US: 2011.

Mayer, John, Peter Salovey, and David Caruso. *Models of Emotional Intelligence: Handbook of Intelligence*. London: Cambridge University Press, 2000.

Montan, Hani. *Thorny Opinion*. Charleston, SC: BookSurge, 2008.

———. *Israel vs. America vs. the World*. Charleston, SC: CreateSpace, 2011.

———. *Death by Choice versus Religious Dogma*. Charleston, SC: CreateSpace, 2012.

———. *Dads Gags*. Charleston, SC: CreateSpace, 2009.

Sachs, Jeffrey. *The Price of Civilisation: Reawakening American Virtue and Prosperity*. New York: Random House, 2012.

Salovey, Peter and John Mayer. "Emotional Intelligence." *Imagination, Cognition, and Personality*. London: 1990.

Smith, Peter. *Bullying at Schools: How Successful Can Intervention Be?* UK: Cambridge, 2004.

Zarit, Steven and Judy Zarit. *Mental Disorders in Older Adults: Fundamentals of Assessment and Treatment*. 2nd edition. New York: Guilford Press, 2011.